NORWAY TRAVEL GUIDE

Must-See Hidden Gems & Scenic Norwegian Attractions

Fred Tovar

Copyright © 2025 Fred Tovar

All rights reserved. No part of this book may be reproduced or transmitted in any form or by any means, electronic or mechanical, including photocopying, recording, or by any information storage and retrieval system, without written permission from the publisher, except in the case of brief quotations embodied in critical articles or reviews.

Disclaimer:

The authors and publisher have made every effort to ensure the accuracy of the information in this book. However, they are not responsible for any errors or omissions, and they disclaim any liability for any damages or losses arising from the use of the information contained herein.

QUICK NOTE

Hey! Before you start reading this guide, there are a few things I need to share with you.

First off, this is the first edition of our guide. We've worked really hard on it, but we know it can get better. Please inform us by leaving a review if you have identified any areas for improvement! Your feedback will help us make future versions even more awesome.

Second, thank you for choosing our travel guide! We are excited to enhance your travel experience with a special bonus: **printable travel journal pages.** These pages are designed to help you document your journey, capture memorable moments, and keep track of your adventures.
To access your printable travel journal pages, simply click on the link or scan the QR code provided on page **195** of this e-book.

Finally, if you enjoy the guide or even feel we could have done something better, do take a moment to leave a review on Amazon. It will help us improve as well as assist other travelers.
Happy travels and enjoyable journaling!

Table of Contents

CHAPTER 1

Why Visit Norway	11
When to Go	12
Getting Here and Around	15

CHAPTER 2

Oslo	19
Bygdøy	22
Sentrum	25
Grünerløkka	37
Aker Brygge	40
Frogner	45
Holmenkollen	50

CHAPTER 3

Bergen	55
Bryggen	59
Sentrum	65
Greater Bergen	71

Table of Contents

CHAPTER 4

Southern Norway	74
Arendal	77
Kristiansand	78
Stavanger	81
Risør	87
Lillesand	87
Sandefjord	90
Kragerø	91

CHAPTER 5

Central Norway	94
Røros	96
Hamar	99
Dombås	103
Otta	105
Ringebu	107
Beitostølen	111
Lillehammer	113
Fagernes	117

CHAPTER 6

Oslofjord	121
Bærum	122
Drøbak	123
Fredrikstad	127
Halden	129

Table of Contents

CHAPTER 7

Western Fjord	131
Åndalsnes	133
Utne	134
Olden	134
Kinsarvik	135
Eidfjord	136
Balestrand	138
Flåm	139
Ålesund	144
Odda	142
Aurland	146
Fjærland	147
Hellesylt	148
Geiranger	149
Kristiansund	152
Loen	153

CHAPTER 8

TOP EXPERIENCE AND ADVENTURES	156
Top Attractions in Norway	156
Outdoor Activities	166

CHAPTER 9

ESSENTIAL TRAVEL INFORMATION	172
Travel Itinerary	175
Norway Travel Cost	180
Tips for Travelers	182
Health and Emergency Contacts	191

WELCOME TO NORWAY

Geography and Location of Norway

Norway, located in Northern Europe, occupies the western portion of the Scandinavian Peninsula. It shares a long eastern border with Sweden, while its northern boundary meets Finland and Russia. To the west and south, Norway is flanked by the Norwegian Sea, the North Sea, and the Skagerrak Strait, giving the country an extensive coastline that stretches over 25,000 kilometers, including its intricate fjords and countless islands.

The terrain is dominated by rugged mountains, expansive plateaus, and deep glacial valleys. The Scandinavian Mountains, also known as the Scandes, run along the country's spine, creating a natural barrier with Sweden. These mountains descend sharply towards the west, forming some of Norway's most iconic fjords, such as Geirangerfjord and Sognefjord, the latter being the longest and deepest in the country.

Central and eastern Norway are characterized by fertile valleys and rolling hills, making the region suitable for agriculture. The Oslofjord region in the southeast is a key hub for population and economic activity, centered around the capital, Oslo. Northern Norway, often referred to as the Arctic region, extends above the Arctic Circle and is home to the Lofoten Islands, dramatic coastal cliffs, and the unique midnight sun phenomenon during summer.

Norway's location provides it with diverse climatic zones. The western coast experiences a maritime climate, with mild winters and cool summers, while inland regions and the far north have a more continental and subarctic climate. The Gulf Stream moderates the climate along the coast, ensuring ice-free ports even during winter.

Norway's geographical diversity also includes over 50,000 islands, many of which are located off the western and northern coasts. The Arctic archipelago of Svalbard, situated midway between mainland Norway and the North Pole, is an integral part of the country and offers a starkly different landscape of glaciers, tundra, and polar wildlife.

The History of Norway

Norway's history dates back to prehistoric times, with evidence of human settlement as early as 10,000 BCE, following the retreat of Ice Age glaciers. These early inhabitants were primarily hunter-gatherers, relying on fishing and hunting for survival. By the Bronze Age (1800-500 BCE), Norway saw advancements in agriculture and trade, as well as the emergence of rock carvings and other cultural artifacts.

The Viking Age (793-1066 CE) is a defining chapter in Norway's history. Norwegian Vikings, known for their seafaring skills, explored, traded, and raided across Europe, establishing settlements as far as Iceland, Greenland, and North America. During this era, Norway transitioned from a collection of small chiefdoms into a unified kingdom under Harald Fairhair in the late 9th century. The Viking period also marked the gradual Christianization of Norway, culminating in the adoption of Christianity as the state religion by King Olaf II (St. Olaf) in the 11th century.

Following the Viking Age, Norway entered a period of political consolidation and cultural development. The 13th century, under King Haakon IV, is often considered a golden age, marked by territorial expansion, a strong monarchy, and flourishing literature, including the Icelandic sagas. However, the Black Death in the mid-14th century devastated Norway, killing a significant portion of the population and weakening its economy and political influence.

In 1397, Norway entered the Kalmar Union with Denmark and Sweden, eventually falling under Danish rule for nearly 400 years. This period, often called the "400-Year Night," saw Norway's status decline, with Copenhagen serving as the political and cultural center. In 1814, following Denmark's defeat in the Napoleonic Wars, Norway entered a brief period of independence before entering a union with Sweden. This union lasted until 1905, when Norway peacefully gained full independence through a referendum.

The 20th century was transformative for Norway. It established itself as a modern, democratic state with significant economic and social reforms. During World War II, Norway was occupied by Nazi Germany from 1940 to 1945, leaving a lasting impact on the nation's collective memory. Post-war reconstruction, combined with the discovery of oil in the North Sea in the 1960s, led to unprecedented economic growth, positioning Norway as one of the world's wealthiest nations.

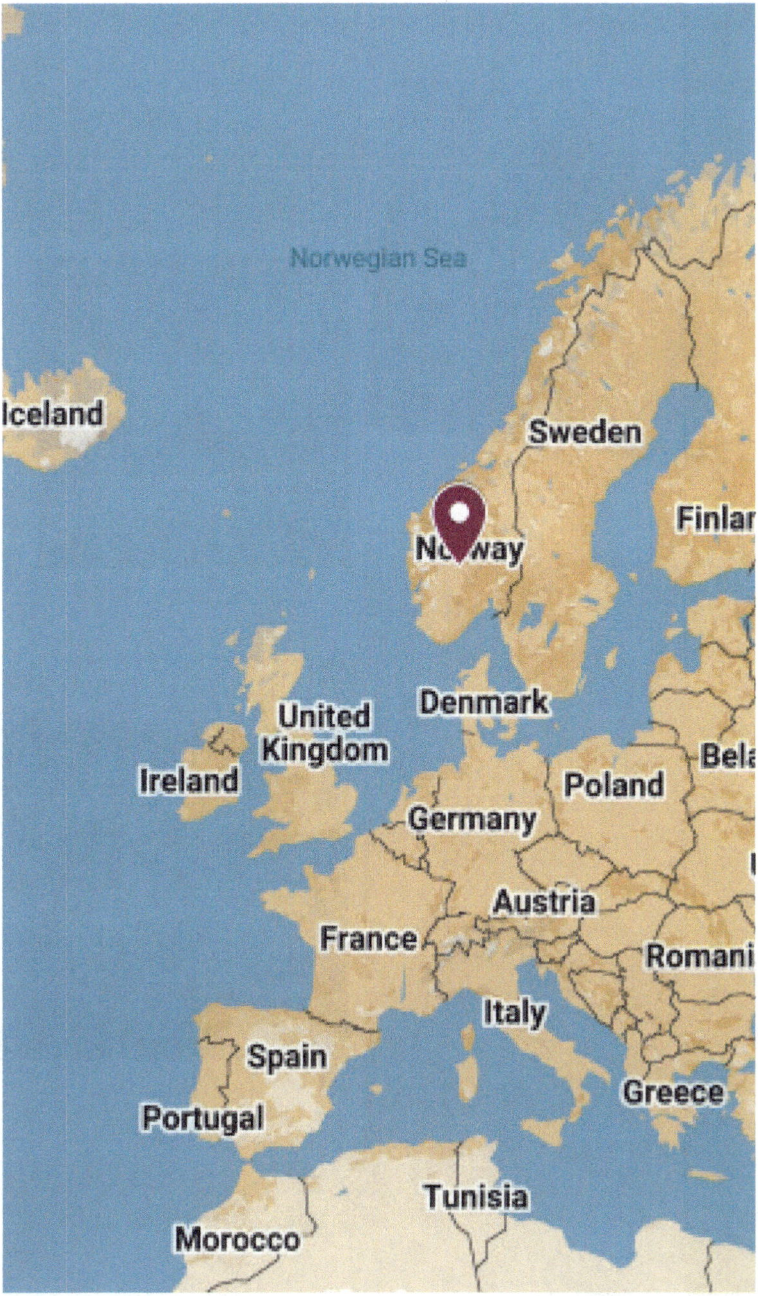

CHAPTER 1

WHY VISIT NORWAY

Norway is not just a place you visit; it's a journey into the extraordinary. This Scandinavian gem offers a symphony of natural wonders that defy expectations. Towering fjords like Geirangerfjord and Nærøyfjord carve dramatic pathways into the land, their sheer cliffs plunging into emerald waters that reflect the majesty above. The midnight sun in summer gifts you endless daylight to explore, while winter unveils the ethereal northern lights—a celestial dance that humbles every observer.

For adventure enthusiasts, Norway is a playground like no other. Trek the jagged peaks of the Lofoten Islands, kayak through serene fjords, or brave the iconic Trolltunga hike for a view that feels like standing on the edge of the world. In the winter months, experience the thrill of dog sledding across snowy tundras or skiing under polar skies in world-class resorts like Hemsedal. The Arctic waters surrounding Norway teem with life, offering unparalleled whale safaris to see orcas and humpbacks in their natural habitat.

Norwegian cuisine is a hidden treasure that tells the story of the land and sea. From fresh Arctic char and reindeer to the traditional flavors of rakfisk (fermented fish) and brown cheese, the food is both simple and profound, rooted in sustainability and seasonality. A visit to a local fish market or dining at a fjord-side restaurant offers a taste of Norway's bounty. And don't miss trying aquavit, the Nordic spirit that warms you in every sense.

Culturally, Norway is a nation deeply connected to its Viking roots and modern-day progressiveness. The cities, such as Oslo and Bergen, blend history and innovation seamlessly. Oslo's Vigeland Sculpture Park and the Munch Museum celebrate creativity, while Bergen's Bryggen Wharf reflects the maritime legacy of the Hanseatic League. Visit quaint stave churches scattered across the countryside, their intricate wooden carvings echoing tales of resilience and devotion.

Above all, Norway is a pioneer in living harmoniously with nature. This is a country that leads by example in sustainability, from its green cities to its protected wilderness areas. Whether it's sailing through untouched fjords, experiencing the quiet beauty of the Arctic wilderness, or simply walking the cobbled streets of a charming fishing village, Norway invites you to slow down and rediscover what it means to truly connect—with the earth, with yourself, and with the moment.

When to Go

Events Throughout the Year in Norway

January
The Polar Night Half-Marathon in Tromsø takes place in early January under a perpetually dark sky, offering a chance to glimpse the northern lights. For details, visit msm.no/en/arrangement/morkertidslopet or call 77-67-33-63. The Tromsø International Film Festival, held during the third week, showcases local and global films on outdoor screens. Learn more at tiff.no/en or contact 77-775-30-90. The Northern Lights Festival in Tromsø features classical music, jazz, opera, and chamber performances. Details at nordlysfestivalen.no/en or 92-09-32-52.

February
Sámi National Day is celebrated on February 6 across Lapland, including Tromsø, with events like reindeer races and lasso-throwing. Visit msm.no/en/arrangement/samisk-uke or call 77-67-33-63. Holmenkollmarsjen, a cross-country ski race near Oslo, happens mid-month. Visit skiforeningen.no/en/kursogarrangement/holmenkollmarsjen or call 22-92-32-00. The Ice Music Festival, featuring instruments made of ice, occurs in early February. Visit icemusicfestivalnorway.no for details. The Røros Winter Fair, a traditional outdoor market since 1854, is held late in the month. Visit rorosmartnan.no or call 72-41-00-00.

March
Borealis, Bergen's experimental arts festival, features exhibitions and screenings in mid-March. Visit borealisfestival.no or call 95-90-53-76. Finnmarksløpet, a dog sled race across northern Norway, starts mid-month.

Visit finnmarkslopet.no or call 900-81-519. The Birkebeinerrennet cross-country ski race runs from Rena to Lillehammer in the third week. Visit birkebeiner.no/en/ski/birkebeinerrennet-54-km or call 41-77-29-00.

April
The Sámi Easter Festival in Karasjok includes ice-fishing contests and reindeer races. Details are available at samieasterfestival.com or by calling 93-22-94-94.

May
On May 17, Norwegians celebrate National Day with parades and festive foods like ice cream and hot dogs. Learn more at visitnorway.com/typically-norwegian/norways-national-day. The Bergen International Festival spans two weeks of performing arts. Visit fib.no/en or call 55-21-06-30.

June
The Midnight Sun Marathon in Tromsø occurs during a sunlit night in late June. Visit msm.no/en or call 77-67-33-63. Sankthansaften, celebrated with bonfires on June 23, is particularly lively in Ålesund. Details at visitnorway.com/media/news-from-norway/sankthans-finds-norway-at-its-brightest-and-most-summery. The Festspillene Nord-Norge in Harstad showcases Northern Norway's culture. Visit festspillnn.no or call 77-04-12-30. Stavanger hosts the Glad Mat food festival, attracting 250,000 visitors. Details at gladmat.no or 51-87-45-78.

July
Moldejazz, Norway's premier jazz festival, occurs in the fjords during the fourth week. Visit moldejazz.no/en or call 71-20-31-50. Riddu Riddu, an indigenous cultural festival, is held in mid-July in the Lyngen Alps. Visit riddu.no/en or call 971-39-493.

August
The Parkenfestivalen in Bodø brings international and local artists during the third week. Visit parkenfestivalen.no or call 978-96-486. The Norwegian International Film Festival in Haugesund closes August with the Amanda Award ceremony. Visit filmfestivalen.no for more details.

September
NuArt, Norway's only street art festival, is hosted in Stavanger. Visit

nuartfestival.no for details. Tromsø's SMAK food festival celebrates northern Norwegian cuisine in mid-September. Visit smakfest.no/en. The Oslo Marathon, Norway's largest, welcomes runners from late September into early October. Visit oslomaraton.no/en or call 900-47-200.

October
Svalbard's Dark Season Blues Festival ends October with live music before months of polar night. Visit svalbardblues.com for more information.

November
Pepperkakebyen Bergen, the largest gingerbread village, opens for the holiday season. Visit pepperkakebyen.org for details.

December
The Røros Christmas Market transforms this UNESCO World Heritage town into a festive destination. Visit julemarkedroros.no or call 72-41-00-00.

Trolltunga, Norway

GETTING THERE AND AROUND

Norway has developed a highly efficient public transportation network that seamlessly integrates buses, trains, and ferries for smooth travel. Connections are carefully timed, ensuring a train's arrival aligns with a ferry's departure. Schedules change seasonally, so it's essential to consult regional tourist offices for updated departure times when planning your journey.

Air Travel in Norway

The primary gateway to Norway is Gardermoen Airport, located 53 kilometers northeast of Oslo. Bergen Airport, 18 kilometers south of the city, is another significant hub, with additional international airports in Kristiansand, Sandefjord, Stavanger, Tromsø, and Trondheim. Most flights to these airports originate within Norway or Europe. Norwegian Airlines and Scandinavian Airlines System (SAS) provide direct flights to Oslo from cities like New York and Los Angeles. Flights from London to Oslo take around 1 hour and 45 minutes, while a trip from New York takes approximately eight hours. Budget carriers like EasyJet, Ryanair, and Wizz Air also operate flights to Oslo from various European cities.

Domestic flights are well-serviced by Norwegian Airlines, SAS, and Widerøe, which covers 42 destinations across the country. Passengers on budget airlines might land at Torp Airport in Sandefjord, located 110 kilometers south of Oslo. For flight schedules, transfers, and parking details, visit Avinor's official website, which manages most Norwegian airports.

Airport Transfers
Airport transfers in Norway are straightforward. Flybussen buses offer frequent departures from the airports to central locations, while Flytoget express trains connect Gardermoen to Oslo Central Station every 10 minutes.

Bergen Light Rail also departs every 10 minutes, linking Bergen Airport to Byparken Station in the city center.

Boat and Ferry Travel

For maritime enthusiasts, Norway offers unparalleled experiences. Hurtigruten, a historic coastal steamer operating since 1893, sails a breathtaking route from Bergen to Kirkenes, near the Russian border. The 12-day journey covers 2,500 nautical miles, stopping at 34 ports. Onboard amenities include cabins, dining facilities, and shops. Tickets for the entire trip or specific segments can be booked directly through Hurtigruten.

Norway's fjords also provide stunning ferry routes, ranging from leisurely scenic trips to thrilling speedboat rides. Ferries play a vital role in connecting coastal communities, especially in the west and north. Car ferries like Lauvvik-Lysebotn often experience queues in summer, making early arrival and advance booking essential. Scenic routes such as Geiranger-Hellesylt are particularly popular with tourists.

International ferry connections are available as well. Color Line operates routes to Kiel, Germany, and Hirtshals, Denmark, while DFDS Scandinavian Seaways offers services to Copenhagen via Helsingborg, Sweden. Ferries also connect Oslo to coastal towns around Oslofjord, a vast waterway extending to the capital.

Bus Travel in Norway

Buses are a practical choice for exploring Norway's smaller regions. Operated by companies such as Nettbuss, a subsidiary of the national railway, and Nor-Way Bussekspress, which serves over 500 destinations, buses offer extensive coverage for most journeys. Many long-distance buses depart from Oslo's central terminal, next to Oslo Central Station. While buses are effective, trains generally provide broader coverage, shorter travel times, and slightly higher fares, making them a preferable option for many travelers.

Driving in Norway

Norway's National Tourist Routes offer drivers 18 stunning scenic drives, spanning over 1,850 kilometers and highlighting the coastal areas and fjords. Popular routes include the Rondane National Tourist Route through the mountains and the Lofoten National Tourist Route in the islands. Southern Norway's cities are within a day's drive of each other, while the northern regions require more planning due to narrow, winding roads and potential weather-related closures, particularly from October to June. Road safety is a priority, with clear signage and laws requiring headlights and seat belts at all times. For assistance, roadside services are available through Norges Automobil-Forbund and Falck Global Assistance.

Car Rentals and Regulations

Car rental policies in Norway often require drivers under 25 to pay a surcharge. Collision and theft coverage may not be included, so check your existing insurance and credit card policies before renting. Drivers with valid licenses from the U.S., Canada, the U.K., Australia, or New Zealand can legally drive in Norway. Be prepared for toll charges when entering cities like Oslo, Bergen, and Trondheim. Automated traffic cameras enforce speed limits, and directional and informational signs are well-marked for navigation.

Cruises in Norway

Cruise ships offer an unparalleled way to explore Norway's iconic fjords and coastal highlights. These cruises often include optional excursions, such as walking tours or bus rides at each port, for an additional fee. Major lines like Celebrity, Princess, Holland America, Costa Cruises, and Viking provide a variety of itineraries, with Viking offering luxurious options. Ports of call range from Bergen in the south to Honningsvåg in the north, showcasing Norway's breathtaking landscapes and cultural heritage.

Train Travel in Norway

Norway's train routes are renowned for their spectacular views. The Flåmsbana, a 20-kilometer journey from Myrdal to Flåm, is a tourist favorite, while the Bergensbanen's seven-hour ride from Oslo to Bergen traverses 180 tunnels and crosses the scenic Hardangervidda plateau. The southern line connects Oslo to Stavanger, and the northern route extends from Trondheim to Bodø. While trains provide exceptional scenery, flying may be necessary for longer journeys, as Stavanger in the south is equidistant from Rome and Norway's northernmost regions.

CHAPTER 2

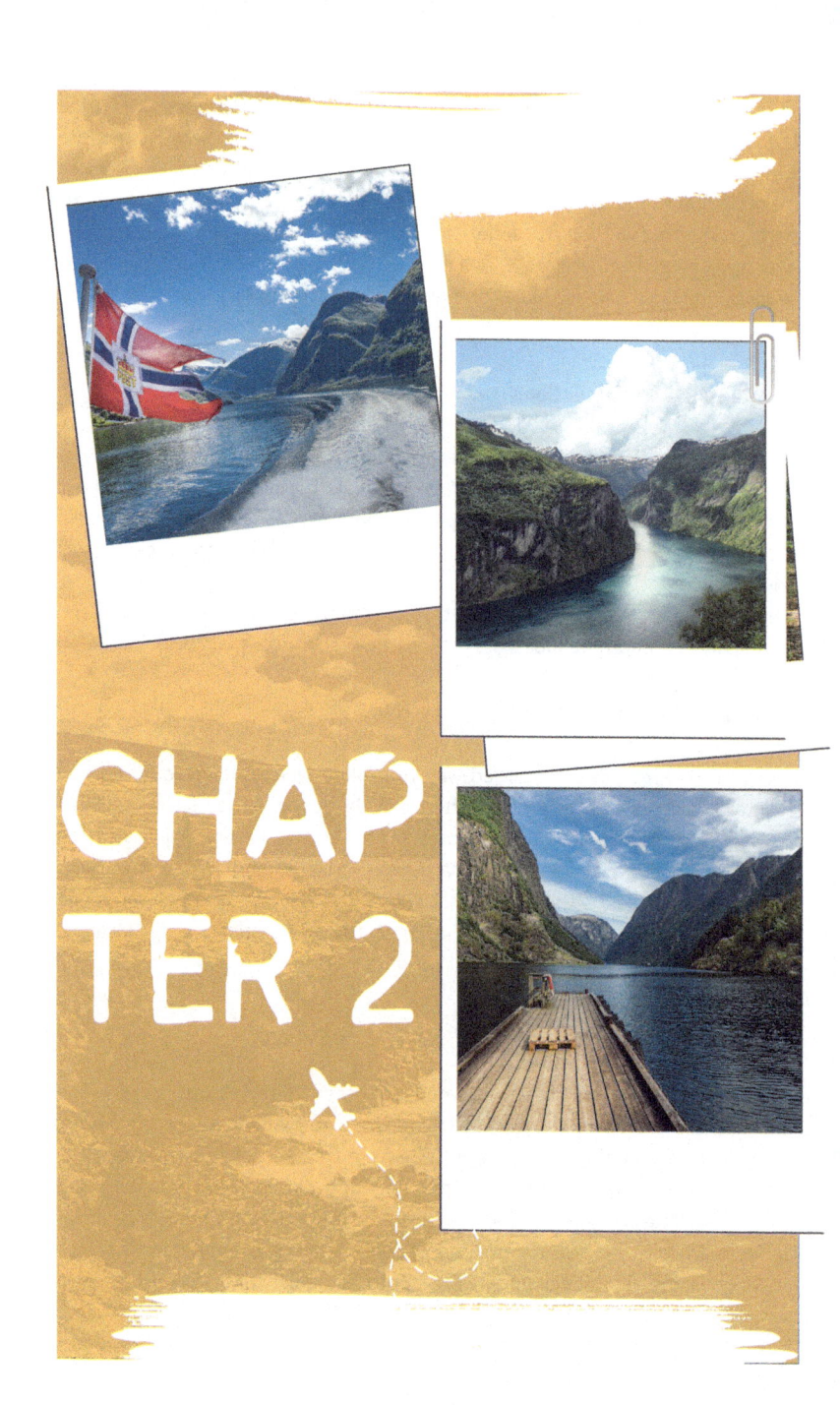

OSLO

What distinguishes Oslo from other European capitals is its extraordinary natural setting. Few cities in the world offer subway access to lush forests, lakes, and hiking trails within their boundaries. However, Oslo is far more than its picturesque landscapes. It boasts a cosmopolitan vibe, internationally acclaimed cultural institutions, a thriving culinary scene attracting global food enthusiasts, and a dynamic nightlife that rivals other Scandinavian capitals.

Once overlooked by travelers, Oslo has emerged as a sought-after destination and serves as a gateway to Norway's stunning landscapes. The city, home to about 1 million residents, has endured numerous challenges over its 1,000-year history. In 1348, a devastating plague halved the population, and in 1624, a catastrophic fire razed much of the city. Rebuilt and renamed Christiania by King Christian IV of Denmark, Oslo steadily grew to become Norway's largest and most economically significant city.

The mid-19th century saw Oslo under Swedish rule, during which King Karl Johan commissioned the construction of the iconic Karl Johans Gate, a vibrant street central to the city's life. Following Norway's independence from Sweden in 1905, Parliament restored the city's original name, Oslo, in 1925. Today, Oslo stands as Norway's political, economic, and cultural hub. Its commitment to sustainability earned it the title of European Eco Capital in 2019, reflecting its leadership in green living and urban innovation.

Planning Your Trip to Oslo

Ideal Time to Visit

Oslo welcomes visitors year-round, with locals embracing the outdoors in every season. Winter offers a unique urban sauna experience, where locals alternate between icy fjord dips and relaxing in floating saunas equipped with personal music systems. Traditional winter activities like city-center ice skating and nearby tobogganing are also popular. However, temperatures can plunge to -15°C (5°F), with limited daylight, so warm clothing and early starts are essential. Summers from May to September bring pleasant weather, with temperatures occasionally reaching 30°C (86°F). During these months, locals flock to fjordside beaches, enjoy their summer cabins, and participate in festivals like the Øyafestivalen music event.

Getting Around Oslo

Air Travel

Oslo Airport, located 45 km (28 miles) north of the city, provides scenic views through its massive windows and boasts an advanced weather system minimizing delays. The Flytoget express train connects the airport to Oslo Central Station in just 20 minutes, with departures every 10 minutes. Alternatively, Flybussen buses offer routes into the city every 30 minutes, taking about 50 minutes. Taxis are available at the airport, but rides can be costly. For budget travelers, smaller airlines land at Torp Airport in Sandefjord, 110 km (68 miles) south of Oslo, with Torp Express Buss services taking nearly two hours to reach the city center. Contacts: Flytoget (+47 23 15 90 00, www.flytoget.no/en); Torp Express Buss (+47 23 00 24 00, www.torp.no/en/transport/bus).

Public Transport

Oslo's comprehensive public transport system includes buses, trams, and trains, with the T-bane subway featuring five lines and 101 stations. Line 1 to Holmenkollen ski jump is a favorite among travelers. An Oslo Pass, starting at NKr 445, offers convenient access to transportation and attractions. Contact: www.ruter.no.

Boat Services

Ferries connect Oslo with ports in Denmark, Germany, and Sweden. Local ferries run from Aker Brygge to harbor islands and Bygdøy, home to major museums, between April and September. Contacts: Color Line (+47 99 56 19 00, www.colorline.com); DFDS Scandinavian Seaways (+47 23 10 68 00, www.dfds.no).

Other Options

Taxis are readily available but expensive, while driving in Oslo is unnecessary due to its compact layout and toll fees of NKr 22-28. Vy trains connect Oslo with the rest of Norway, offering upgraded services like business-class seats. Contact: www.vy.no.

Shopping in Oslo

Oslo is the ideal destination for Norwegian goods, including hand-knitted sweaters, reindeer products, and hiking gear. Sentrum hosts high-end boutiques and department stores, while Grünerløkka and Frogner feature antiques and thrift shops. Prices for handmade items like knitwear are regulated, and most shops close on Sundays. Look for signs like "salg" and "tilbud" for discounts.

Exploring Oslo

Walking and biking tours are popular ways to experience Oslo's highlights, with options ranging from spooky haunts to Viking history. Oslo City and Nature Walks offer guided tours along rivers, while Our Way Tours focuses on alternative neighborhoods. Stromma provides hop-on/hop-off buses and boat tours, while Båtservice Sightseeing offers themed fjord cruises. Contacts: Our Way Tours (+47 23 65 16 60, www.ourwaytours.com); Stromma (+47 95 99 60 00, www.stromma.com/en-no/oslo); Båtservice Sightseeing (+47 23 35 68 90, www.nyc.no/boatservice-sightseeing).

Visitor Information

Visit Oslo provides comprehensive travel assistance from their office at Østbanehallen, near Oslo Central Station. Contact: (+47 23 10 62 00, www.visitoslo.com).

Bygdøy

Located southwest of Oslo's city center, the Bygdøy Peninsula houses many of Norway's most iconic historical attractions. The Vikingskipshuset showcases ancient Viking ships, drawing visitors from around the world. Oscarshall Slott Åd, a charming pink castle nestled in the trees, once served as a royal summer retreat. The area also features the current royal family's summer residence, a large white house nearby. The Norsk Folkemuseum adds to the appeal with its black stave church and farm exhibits, offering insight into Norway's cultural heritage.

Navigating Bygdøy

Reaching Bygdøy is most enjoyable between May and September via a ferry from Pier 3 behind City Hall. The ferry stops at Dronningen, a short walk from the Folk Museum. For year-round access, Bus No. 30 provides a convenient option, with a travel time of 10 to 20 minutes.

Attractions

Bygdø Kongsgård (Bygdøy Royal Estate)
The Bygdøy Royal Estate, part of the Norwegian Folk Museum, is a functioning organic farm spanning nearly 500 acres. Owned by Norway's royal family, it features horseback riding lessons and opportunities for children to interact with barnyard animals. The estate includes the manor house, which serves as the king's official summer residence and was constructed in 1733 by Count Christian Rantzau. Opening hours vary depending on the royal family's presence. Visit bygdokongsgard.no for details.

Frammuseet (Fram Museum)
The Fram Museum highlights the legendary Polar ship Fram, used by explorer Roald Amundsen when he reached the South Pole in 1911. Built in 1892, this vessel has ventured farther north and south than any other. Visitors can explore the ship's interior, including the captain's quarters with sealskin jackets and expedition relics. The museum also showcases artifacts from Arctic expeditions. Located at Bygdøynesvn 36, it's open year-round. For information, call 22-13-52-80 or visit frammuseum.no.

Kon-Tiki Museet (Kon-Tiki Museum)
The Kon-Tiki Museum celebrates Thor Heyerdahl's daring voyages, including his 1947 expedition from Peru to Polynesia on the balsa raft Kon-Tiki. Exhibits include his reed boat Ra II, artifacts from Peru and Polynesia, and a film room. The museum is located at Bygdøynesvn 36 and operates daily from 10 AM to 6 PM. Call 23-08-67-67 or visit kon-tiki.no for details.

Norsk Folkemuseum (Norwegian Museum of Cultural History)
This expansive open-air museum offers a journey through Norway's history with its authentic buildings, including a stave church from 1200 and sod-roofed farmhouses. Displays feature national costumes, Sámi traditional attire, dragon-style carvings, and rosemaling. Located at Museumsvn 10, the museum offers a summer program of folk dancing, guided tours, and tastings. Tickets cost 160 NOK. Contact 22-12-37-00 or visit norskfolkemuseum.no.

Norsk Maritimt Museum (Norwegian Maritime Museum)
The Norwegian Maritime Museum showcases the nation's maritime heritage through ship models, fishing displays, and the Arctic vessel Gjøa. Visitors can also watch The Ocean: A Way of Life, a film exploring Norway's coastal history. The museum, located at Bygdøynesvn 37, charges 120 NOK for admission. For more information, call 22-12-37-00 or visit marmuseum.no.

Oscarshall Slott (Oscarshall Palace)
Built in the mid-19th century for King Oscar I, Oscarshall Palace features a Gothic-style castle, park, pavilion, and artworks by Norwegian artists. The grounds include a stage and a fountain. Located on Oscarshallveien, the palace is closed October through May and on Sundays and Mondays during summer. For details, call 91-70-23-61 or visit royalcourt.no.

Senter for Studier av Holocaust og Livssynsminoriteter (Center for Studies of the Holocaust and Religious Minorities)
Housed in the scenic Villa Grande, this museum offers a profound exhibition on the Holocaust, including the impact on Norway's Jewish community. Located at Huk Aveny 56, it charges 70 NOK for admission. Call 22-84-21-00 or visit hlsenteret.no for details.

Vikingskipshuset (Viking Ship Museum)
The Viking Ship Museum exhibits three Viking ships—Gokstad, Oseberg, and Tune—dating back to AD 800. These well-preserved vessels were unearthed

from burial mounds and contain household items, tapestries, and animal remains. The museum, located at Huk Aveny 35, is open year-round. Tickets cost 100 NOK. Visit khm.uio.no or call 22-13-52-80 for more information.

Restaurants

Kafe Villa Grande
This villa offers Scandinavian dishes, from sandwiches to grilled fish, with a garden perfect for sunny days. Seasonal mains cost 565 NOK. Located at Huk Aveny 56, Bygdøy. Call 67-10-99-70 or visit sult.no.

Lanternen
Enjoy Scandinavian meals, including pizzas and shellfish, with fjord views from a 1920s dockside terrace. Mains average 180 NOK. Find it at Huk Aveny 2, Bygdøy. Call 22-43-78-38 or visit restaurantlanternen.no.

Lille Herbern
This island spot serves shellfish platters with scenic fjord views, accessible by boat year-round. Located at Herbernveien 1, Bygdøy. Call 22-44-97-00 or visit lilleherbern.no.

A Tramway in Oslo

The Royal Palace in Oslo

Sentrum

Oslo's downtown area is a compact hub with a concentration of shops, restaurants, clubs, and notable landmarks like the Royal Palace and Parliament Building. The city boasts world-class museums, including the National Museum, Munch Museum, and Viking Museum, making it an engaging cultural destination. Its diverse neighborhoods offer a mix of quiet charm and lively streets, creating a dynamic urban experience.

Navigating Oslo

Navigating Oslo is simple, with its compact layout complemented by public transportation accessible with an Oslo Pass, covering buses, trams, trains, and the subway. While some hills make walking or biking challenging, the system is efficient, with features like USB chargers on trams.

Safety

Oslo is considered one of the safest capitals globally, though standard precautions apply when walking alone at night. Despite its calm reputation, it is still a bustling city, and awareness is essential in any urban environment.

Attractions

Nasjonalmuseet (National Museum)
The National Museum, reopened in 2022, is the largest art museum in the Nordic region. Located near the waterfront, its modern structure features a rooftop hall longer than the Royal Palace, offering views of Oslo City Hall, Akershus Fortress, and the Oslofjord. The Edvard Munch collection includes The Dance of Life, an oil version of The Scream, and self-portraits. Works by Hans Gude, Adolph Tidemand, Monet, Renoir, Van Gogh, and Gauguin are also displayed, alongside Nordic 20th-century art. The museum includes landscaped garden seating and hosts special events year-round. Visit at Brynjulf Bulls Plass, with details at www.nasjonalmuseet.no or call 21-98-20-00.

Nationaltheatret (National Theater)
This Neoclassical theater, established in 1899, features statues of Norwegian playwrights Henrik Ibsen and Bjørnstjerne Bjørnson. Performances are primarily in Norwegian, but guided English tours can be pre-booked for NKr 90, offering insight into the lives of these literary greats. Located at Johanne Dybwads Plass 1, more details are available at www.nationaltheatret.no or by calling 22-00-14-00.

Nobels Fredssenter (Nobel Peace Center)
Located by the harbor, the Nobel Peace Center celebrates laureates and their work with high-tech installations featuring 1,000 fiber-optic lights. Visitors can explore Alfred Nobel's achievements through interactive displays and documentaries. Family-friendly activities include peace-themed workshops, and the museum hosts rotating exhibitions such as humanitarian spotlights. Admission is NKr 120, and the center is closed Mondays from October to April. Visit Brynjulf Bulls Plass or www.nobelpeacecenter.org for more information, or call 483-01-000.

Oslo Domkirke (Oslo Cathedral)
Consecrated in 1697, Oslo Cathedral is known for its original pulpit, altarpiece, and organ with acanthus carvings. Ceiling murals by Hugo Louis Mohr and stained-glass windows by Emanuel Vigeland add to its charm. In the 19th century, its bell tower served as a fire department lookout, which can still be toured by booking in advance. Located at Karl Johans Gate 11, further details are available at www.kirken.no or by calling 23-62-90-10. Entry is free.

Rådhuset (City Hall)
Oslo's City Hall hosts the annual Nobel Peace Prize ceremony on December 10. Its walls feature museum-quality frescoes, while the Banquet Hall displays royal portraits. Free guided tours are offered in June and July, starting in the Main Hall. The City Hall Gallery, accessed via the harbor, showcases special exhibits year-round. On special occasions, the Central Hall is illuminated by 60 spotlights. Visit at Rådhusplassen 1, with details at https://www.oslo.kommune.no/radhuset/#gref or call 23-46-12-00. Entry is free.

Oslo Pass
The Oslo Pass, available at www.visitoslo.com/en/activities-and-attractions/oslo-pass, is ideal for exploring Oslo's attractions. It comes in 24-

hour (NKr 445), 48-hour (NKr 655), and 72-hour (NKr 820) options. The pass covers entry to most galleries, museums, Akershus Fortress, the Holmenkollen Ski Museum, and Vigeland Sculpture Park. It also includes unlimited use of public transportation within the two downtown zones and regional trains, plus discounts at various restaurants and cafés.

Royal Palace Guard Ceremony
The Royal Palace features a 40-minute guard-changing ceremony accompanied by the Norwegian Military Band. This free event takes place daily at 1:30, regardless of the weather. Located at Slottsplassen 1, additional details are available at www.kongehuset.no or by calling 81-53-31-33. Advance tickets to other palace events cost NKr 165, with any remaining tickets sold at the entrance for NKr 125.

Stortinget (Norwegian Parliament)
Built in 1866, Norway's Parliament building offers a glimpse into the country's political history. Public access is limited to guided tours available every Saturday throughout the year, with additional tours in summer. These informative one-hour tours, offered in English and Norwegian, are free and operate on a first-come, first-served basis as reservations cannot be made in advance. Tours begin at the Akersgata entrance. Located at Karl Johans Gate 22, more details can be found at www.stortinget.no or by calling 23-31-30-50.

Restaurants

Asylet
Homemade Norwegian dishes like smørrebrød and karbonade served in a historic 1730s building. Located at Grønland 28, Oslo. Main dishes average NKr150. Visit www.asylet.no or call 22-17-09-39.

Atlas Brasserie
Stylish brasserie offering seafood platters and tomahawk steak. Located at Amerikalinjen Hotel, Jernbanetorget 2, Oslo. Main dishes average NKr250. Visit www.amerikalinjen.com or call 21-40-59-00.

Brasserie France
French classics like steak tartare and bouillabaisse in a Parisian-style setting. Located at Øvre Slottsgate 16, Oslo. Main dishes average NKr300. Visit www.brasseriefrance.no or call 23-10-01-65.

J2
Modern Korean kitchen serving creative snacks and mains. Located at Pilestredet 63A, Oslo. Main dishes average NKr200. Visit www.j2restaurant.no.

Kafeteria August
Scandinavian dishes made with fresh local ingredients. Located at Universitetsgata 9, Oslo. Main dishes average NKr150. Visit www.kafeteriaaugust.no or call 920-25-580.

Kaffistova
Traditional Norwegian food like raspeballer and boknafisk in a casual setting. Located at Rosenkrantz gt. 8, Oslo. Main dishes average NKr180. Visit www.kaffistova.com or call 21-41-00.

Katla
Eclectic cuisine blending Nordic, Asian, and Latin flavors. Located at Universitetsgata 12, Oslo. Main dishes average NKr895. Visit www.katlaoslo.no or call 22-69-50-00.

Klosteret
Nordic-Germanic cuisine with wine pairings in a candlelit cloister setting. Located at Fredensborgveien 13, Oslo. Main dishes average NKr300. Visit www.klosteret.no or call 23-35-49-00.

Konoji
Cozy sake bar and izakaya offering casual Japanese dishes. Located at Trondheimsveien 16, Oslo. Main dishes average NKr250. Visit www.konojioslo.no.

Kulturhuset
Vegetarian-friendly eatery with a casual all-day menu. Located at Youngs gt. 6, Oslo. Main dishes average NKr120. Visit www.kulturhusetioslo.no.

Lobbybar
Creative Norwegian bistro with small plates and local cheeses. Located at Radisson Blu Scandinavia Hotel, Oslo. Main dishes average NKr300. Visit www.26north.no or call 23-29-34-25.

Mamma Pizza
Authentic sourdough pizzas with gluten-free options. Located at Dronningens gt. 22, Oslo. Main dishes average NKr180. Visit www.mammapizza.no or call 915-11-841.

Oslo Street Food
Food hall with 16 international food stands. Located at Torggata 16, Oslo. Main dishes average NKr150. Visit www.oslo-streetfood.no.

Palmen Restaurant
Luxurious bistro with afternoon tea under a glass ceiling. Located at Karl Johans gt. 31, Oslo. Main dishes average NKr265. Visit www.grand.no or call 23-21-20-00.

Pink Fish Grensen
Creative salmon-based dishes like poké bowls and hot pots. Located at Grensen 17, Oslo. Main dishes average NKr120. Visit www.pinkfish.no or call 45-85-50-27.

Sentralen
Scandinavian cuisine with organic ingredients and innovative dishes. Located at Upper Slottsgate 3, Oslo. Main dishes average NKr655. Visit www.sentralenrestaurant.no or call 22-33-22-33.

Theatercafeen
Historic eatery serving Norwegian classics and desserts. Located at Stortingsgt. 24-26, Oslo. Main dishes average NKr300. Visit www.theatercafeen.no or call 22-82-40-50.

The Top
Panoramic dining with Nordic cuisine and tasting menus. Located at Radisson Blu Plaza Hotel, Oslo. Main dishes average NKr330. Visit www.34th.no or call 22-05-80-34.

Fragrance of the Heart
This café serves organic coffee alongside a variety of vegetarian and vegan dishes, plus tempting desserts. Enjoy live music in a cozy setting. Main: NKr210. Nansens pl. 2, Sentrum.
www.fragrance.no | Nationaltheatret.

Pascal
A French-inspired brasserie offering croque monsieur, quiche, and delicious pastries. Known for gluten-free options and a relaxed atmosphere. Main: NKr190. Henrik Ibsens gt. 36, Sentrum.
www.pascal.no | Nationaltheatret.

Tullin's
Tullin's, popular with students, offers a casual vibe with mismatched chairs and quirky decor, serving comfort food like pizza and burgers. Main: NKr175. Tullins gt. 2, Sentrum.
www.tullins.no | Nationaltheatret.

Hotels

Amerikalinjen Hotel
A stylish boutique hotel housed in the former Norwegian America Line headquarters, offering a gym, sauna, and room-service cocktails. Rooms from: NKr2092. Jernbanetorget 2, Oslo.
www.amerikalinjen.com | No meals.

Clarion Hotel The Hub
A business hotel with a modern design, top restaurants, and a focus on sustainability. Conveniently located near the central station. Rooms from: NKr1200. Gunnerusgt. 3, Sentrum.
www.nordicchoicehotels.com | Jernbanetorget.

Clarion Hotel Oslo
Featuring a mix of marble, glass, and stylish furnishings, this hotel offers spacious rooms near the fjord and Munchmuseet. Rooms from: NKr1500. Eufemias gate 15, Oslo.
www.nordicchoicehotels.no | Jernbanetorget.

Comfort Hotel Grand Central
Eco-friendly with a modern design, located behind the central train station. Rooms with bathtubs and practical design. Rooms from: NKr1200. Jernbanetorget 1, Sentrum.
www.nordicchoicehotels.no | Jernbanetorget.

Comfort Hotel Karl Johan
A courtyard hotel offering eco-friendly amenities and a bistro. Located along Karl Johan for a quieter stay in a busy area. Rooms from: NKr1200. Karl Johans gt. 12, Sentrum.
www.nordicchoicehotels.com | Jernbanetorget.

Comfort Hotel Xpress Central Station
A budget-friendly hotel popular with young travelers, featuring self-service check-in and a welcoming atmosphere. Rooms from: NKr900. Møllergata 26, Sentrum.
www.nordicchoicehotels.no | Jernbanetorget.

Grand Hotel
A luxury hotel with a Beaux Arts entrance, offering elegant rooms, town square views, and a stunning spa. Rooms from: NKr2000. Karl Johans gt. 31, Sentrum.
www.grand.no | Stortinget.

Hotel Continental
A historic hotel blending modern design with eco-friendly features, attracting both business travelers and tourists. Rooms from: NKr1800. Stortingsgt. 24–26, Sentrum.
www.hotelcontinental.no | Nationaltheatret.

Nightlife

Andre til Høyre
A stylish bar offering Burgundy and sparkling wines in an elegant atmosphere, perfect for entertaining.
Youngs gt. 19, Sentrum.
www.andretilhoyre.no | Jernbanetorget.

Angst
A quirky bar with neon lights and eclectic furniture, offering live music and a spacious backyard for weekend parties.
Torggata 11, Sentrum. | Jernbanetorget.

Bar Robinet
Known for late-night cocktails and a diverse drink menu, Bar Robinet is located near a popular music venue.
Mariboes gt. 7, Sentrum.
www.barrobinet.com | Stortinget.

Bibliotekbaren og Vinterhaven
Hotel Bristol's Library Bar and Winter Garden offer live piano music in a sophisticated setting, perfect for quiet moments.
IVs gt. 7, Sentrum.
www.thonhotels.com | Stortinget.

Crowbar and Bryggeri
Oslo's largest microbrewery offering hearty pub fare and a rotating selection of beers in a friendly, lively atmosphere. Torggata 32, Sentrum.
www.crowbryggeri.com | Jernbanetorget.

Performing Arts

Fotogalleriet
Located at Møllergata 34, Sentrum, Fotogalleriet is a renowned photography gallery celebrating diverse voices. Closed Mondays, Tuesdays, and July. Admission free. Visit fotogalleriet.no or call P22-20-32-32.

Oslo's Nonstop Festival
Oslo Biennalen runs from 2019-2024, with art showcased in public spaces across the city. Performances occur at various locations like the Opera House and Central Station. Visit oslobiennalen.no.

Gamle Logen
A charming venue for classical music, jazz, and more, located at Grev Wedels Pl., Sentrum. Visit gamlelogen.no or call P22-33-44-70 for event details.

Oslo Konserthus
Home to the Oslo Philharmonic, this venue hosts classical, jazz, and ballet performances. Located at Munkedamsveien 14, Sentrum. Visit oslokonserthus.no or call P23-11-31-11.

Shopping

Basarhallene
Located behind Oslo Domkirke, this Neo-Romanesque arcade offers Norwegian glass and crystal. Visit Sentrum, open daily.

Brocante
A hidden gem at Stensberggata 19, Sentrum, offering antiques from the 19th and 20th centuries. Closed Mondays and Fridays.

Kunstnernes Hus
Exhibiting contemporary art and hosting the Autumn Exhibition, this gallery has a bar and bookstore. Located at Wergelandsvn. 17, Sentrum. Visit kunstnerneshus.no or call P22-85-34-10.

Litteraturhuset
A café, restaurant, and bookstore in the House of Literature located at Wergelandsveien 29, Sentrum. Visit litteraturhuset.no or call P22-95-55-30.

Norli
A large bookstore offering English volumes, located at Universitetsgt. 22-24, Sentrum. Visit norli.no or call P22-00-43-00.

Norlis Antiquarian
This antiquarian bookstore at Universitetsgata 18, Sentrum, is filled with rare

first editions. Visit daily.

Tanum

Located at Karl Johans gt. 37-41, Sentrum, Tanum specializes in books on arts, health, and travel. Visit tanum.no or call P22-47-87-30.

Clothing

Fjong

Rent sustainable designer fashion for four days. Located online, Fjong offers stylish options for travelers. Visit fjong.com.

FWSS

Located at Prinsens gt. 22, Sentrum, FWSS offers simple, timeless fashion pieces. Visit fallwinterspringsummer.com.

Dramatic Northern Lights Aurora In Norway

Mette Møller
A women's fashion brand emphasizing sustainability, located at Prinsens gt. 10, Sentrum. Visit mettemoller.no or call P45-85-10-21.

Norway Shop
Found at Fridtjof Nansens Pl. 9, Sentrum, Norway Shop stocks sweaters and blanket coats. Visit norwayshop.com.

Tom Wood
A contemporary brand offering jewelry, eyewear, and apparel, located at Kirkegata 20, Sentrum. Visit tomwoodproject.com.

UFF Vintage
Located at Prinsens gt. 2B, Sentrum, this store offers second-hand clothing for men, women, and children. Visit uffnorge.org.

Household Items

Heimen Husfliden
Located at Rosenkrantz' gt. 20, Sentrum, this store offers handmade ceramics and textiles. Call P22-42-35-55 for more details.

Norway Designs
Stocking Scandinavian art glass and ceramics, Norway Designs is located at Lille Grensen 7, Sentrum. Visit norwaydesigns.no.

Jewelry

David-Andersen
Located at Karl Johans gt. 20, Sentrum, this goldsmith offers stunning silver and gold jewelry. Visit david-andersen.no.

Hasla
A family-run jewelry business inspired by Norway's natural wonders, located at Markveien 54, Grünerløkka. Visit haslajewelry.com.

Heyerdahl
A sleek jeweler at Karl Johans gt. 37B, Sentrum, offering watches and jewelry. Visit heyerdahl.no.

Juvelér Langaard
This family-run business at Stortingsgaten 22, Sentrum, creates one-of-a-kind jewelry with precious metals. Visit langaard.no.

Sugar Shop Smykkestudio
This workshop and gallery at Sentrum offers unique Norwegian jewelry. Visit sugarshop.no.

Shopping Centers

GlasMagasinet
Located at Stortorvet 9, Sentrum, this chic department store offers handcrafted glass and pewter items. Visit glasmagasinet.no.

Oslo City
A shopping center near Oslo Central Station, offering various shops. Located at Stenersgaten 1, Sentrum. Visit city.steenstrom.no.

Paleet
A high-end shopping arcade between the Parliament and Royal Palace at Karl Johans gt. 37-43, Sentrum. Visit paleet.no.

Steen and Strøm
A traditional mall on Nedre Slottsgate 8, Sentrum, featuring high-end Scandinavian retailers.

Activities

Viking Biking
Located at Akershusstranda 31, Sentrum, Viking Biking offers bike rentals, helmets, and sightseeing tours. Maps are available for those exploring independently. For details, visit vikingbikingoslo.com, or call P412-66-496.

KOK Sauna
KOK Sauna offers a floating sauna experience on the fjords near the Snøhetta Opera House and Munch Museum. Enjoy up to two hours of relaxation with up to 10 people, including a sauna master-led session with aromatherapy. The sauna is available at two locations: Aker Brygge and Langkaia. For bookings, visit koknorge.no or call P34-00-522.

Grünerløkka

Grünerløkka, once a working-class neighborhood north of the city center, has transformed into a vibrant area filled with trendy bars, cafés, and eateries. Often compared to New York's Greenwich Village, this lively district is particularly popular among young people, offering a mix of cultural experiences and urban energy.

Attractions

Galleri Heer
Galleri Heer is an arts center showcasing a variety of artistic expressions, including painting, drawing, photography, sculpture, and graphics. It has been a part of the Oslo art scene for over four decades, featuring works from artists of all ages and backgrounds. The gallery is located at Seilduksgata 4B, Oslo, and is closed on Mondays and Tuesdays. For more details, visit galleriheer.no or call P97-62-04-89.

Galleri Schaeffers Gate 5
Known for its intimate atmosphere, Galleri Schaeffers Gate 5 is a performance venue that hosts readings, art installations, and concerts. Housed in an elegant 1890s tenement building at Schaeffers Gate 5, Grünerløkka, the space offers a unique blend of history and modern art. For more information, visit schaeffersgate5.no or call P452-18-078.

Restaurants

Bass
Located at Grünerløkka 26, Bass serves Scandinavian tapas in a lively setting. Average main: NKr150. Visit bassoslo.no or call P48-24-14-89. Closed Mondays.

Kontrast
Kontrast at Maridalsveien 15 offers New Nordic tasting menus with wine pairings. Average main: NKr2500. Visit restaurant-kontrast.no or call P21-60-01-01. Closed Sundays.

Markveien Mat og Vinhus
This French bistro at Torvbakkgata 12 serves homemade cheesecake and hearty dishes. Average main: NKr310. Visit markveien.no or call P22-37-22-97. Closed Sundays.

Mathallen
Mathallen at Vulkan 5 features 30+ vendors offering diverse food. Average main: NKr150. Visit mathallenoslo.no or call P22-40-40-00. Closed Mondays.

Mucho Mas
Mucho Mas at Thorvald Meyers gt. 36 offers big portions of spicy Mexican food. Average main: NKr200. Visit muchomas.no or call P22-37-16-09.

Munchies
Munchies at Thorvald Meyers gt. 36A serves organic burgers and fries. Average main: NKr105. Visit munchies.no.

New Anarkali
Located at Markveien 42, New Anarkali offers Punjabi dishes. Average main: NKr200. Visit newanarkali.no or call P22-20-04-21.

Tijuana
Tijuana at Thorvald Meyers gt. 61 serves tacos and margaritas. Average main: NKr200. Visit tijuana.no or call P900-77-191.

Villa Paradiso
Villa Paradiso at Olaf Ryes pl. 8 serves wood-fired Neapolitan pizzas. Average main: NKr180. Visit villaparadiso.no or call P22-35-40-60.

Kaffebrenneriet avd Olaf Ryes Plass
Kaffebrenneriet at Thorvald Meyers gt. 55 offers great coffee and snacks. Average main: NKr160. Visit kaffebrenneriet.no or call P22-46-13-90.

Hotels

Scandic Vulkan
Located at Maridalsveien 13, this contemporary hotel is close to restaurants, shopping, and the Akerselva River. Rooms from NKr1200. Visit scandichotels.com/vulkan or call P21-05-71-00. Breakfast available.

Nightlife

Aku-Aku
This vibrant tiki bar at Thorvald Meyers gt. 32 offers tropical drinks with fruit. Visit akuaku.no or call P22-71-75-71.

Bar Boca
Bar Boca at Meyers gt. 30 serves delicious cocktails in a cozy, mysterious space. Visit boca.no or call P22-04-13-77.

Bettola
This vintage cocktail lounge at Trondheimsveien 2 brings the golden age of Italian cinema to Oslo. Call P465-57-776.

Couch
Couch at Thorvald Meyers gt. 33C serves creative cocktails and food in a stylish setting. Visit couchoslo.no or call P22-37-.

Khartoum Bar
Khartoum Bar at Bernt Ankers gt. 17 blends Middle Eastern, African, and European cultures with live music. Call P922-32-273. Closed Mon-Wed.

Parkteatret
Parkteatret at Olaf Ryes pl. 11 hosts live music in an atmospheric Art Deco venue. Visit parkteatret.no or call P22-35-63-00.

Schouskjelleren
This microbrewery at Trondheimsveien 2 offers over 60 beers. Visit schouskjelleren.no or call P21-38-.

Blå
Blå at Brennerivn. 9C is a popular live music venue for jazz, electronica, and hip-hop. Visit blaaoslo.no.

Shopping

Frøken Dianas Salonger
This boutique at Markveien 56 offers vintage fashion, jewelry, and accessories. Visit frokendianassalonger.no or call P467-60-711.

Probat
Probat at Meyers gt. 54 offers cool Norwegian T-shirts. Visit probat.no or call P22-35-20-70.

Velouria Vintage
Velouria Vintage at Thorvald Meyers gt. 34 features '60s and '70s clothes and accessories. Visit velouriavintage.no or call P909-75-191.

Aker Brygge

Oslo is a city full of diverse attractions that blend history, modernity, art, and nature, creating an experience that's both vibrant and multifaceted. From world-renowned museums and architectural wonders to historical landmarks and serene parks, the city caters to all tastes. The following list highlights the essential spots to explore in Oslo for a deeper understanding of its culture and charm.

Attractions

Akershus Fortress
Situated in the heart of Oslo, Akershus Fortress offers a rich historical experience with its green gardens and panoramic views. Visitors can explore the fortress and its surroundings using the Fortress Trail Map, which can be picked up at the visitor center or downloaded from akershusfestning.no. While entry to the fortress grounds is free, the Akershus Slott section has an admission fee of NKr 100. The fortress is sometimes closed for private events, and dates for closures are listed on the website. For further inquiries, contact P23-09-39-17.

Astrup Fearnley Museum of Modern Art
Located across the pedestrian bridge from Aker Brygge, the Astrup Fearnley Museum of Modern Art is an architectural masterpiece designed by Renzo Piano. The museum, housed in three distinct pavilions beneath a massive glass roof, offers contemporary art exhibitions from renowned global artists. The building itself is an artwork, resembling a large, billowing sail. Admission to the museum costs NKr 130, and it is closed on Mondays. Visitors can explore the exhibits and enjoy the views of the Oslo fjord. For more information, visit afmuseet.no or call P22-93-60-60.

Munch Museum

The Munch Museum is a must-visit for art lovers, housing the world's largest collection of Edvard Munch's works, including multiple versions of his iconic The Scream. Located at Munchs pl. 1 in Sentrum, the museum not only displays permanent exhibitions but also hosts changing art shows, making it a dynamic cultural experience. The museum's design allows for incredible indoor and outdoor views of the fjord and the surrounding new district. A café and bistro serve a variety of meals and drinks, offering a perfect spot to relax after exploring the museum. Admission fees and hours can be found on munchmuseet.no, and for inquiries, call P23-49-35-00.

Norway's Resistance Museum

The Norway's Resistance Museum, located at Kvadraturen 21, tells the gripping story of the Norwegian resistance during WWII. The museum is housed in an old ammunition depot, and visitors can explore exhibits filled with photos, documents, and personal stories from the war. Artifacts such as striped prison uniforms and homemade weapons provide insight into the courage and struggles of the resistance. Every year, veterans gather here to commemorate Norway's liberation. Admission is NKr 60, and more information can be found on kultur.forsvaret.no, or by calling P23-09-31-38.

Oslo Opera House

A true masterpiece of modern architecture, the Oslo Opera House sits gracefully on the edge of the Oslo fjord at Kirsten Flagstads pl. 1. Designed by Snøhetta, the white marble and glass building slopes toward the water, offering stunning views of the surrounding mountains, fjord, and city. The venue hosts the Norwegian National Opera and Ballet, and it regularly features performances across a range of genres, from opera to ballet and theater. The acoustics are world-class, and the building's design offers both indoor and outdoor spaces to enjoy the scenic beauty. A guided tour is available for NKr 120. The bistro restaurant is a highlight, serving seafood and wine to make the visit even more memorable. For more details, visit operaen.no or call P21-42-21-21.

Tjuvholmen Bystrand

Tjuvholmen Bystrand, located at Tjuvholmen, offers a peaceful retreat on the waterfront. Though the "beach" is more of a park with gravel at the water's edge, it's a beautiful area to enjoy the outdoors and take in the scenic views. The water is cold, so it's not ideal for swimming, but it's a great spot for a relaxing walk or picnic. The area is free to visit and open to the public, providing a calm break in the middle of Oslo's urban setting.

Tjuvholmen Sculpture Park

Located just outside the Astrup Fearnley Museum, the Tjuvholmen Sculpture Park is an open-air art gallery by the water. Designed by Renzo Piano, this park features a range of contemporary sculptures set against the backdrop of the Oslo fjord. It's a popular spot for locals, especially during warm summer days when people come to picnic and enjoy the views. Admission is free, and the park is open year-round. For more details, visit afmuseet.no or call P22-93-60-60.

Restaurants

Amazonia by BAR

Located at 6 Tjuvholmen, Amazonia by BAR offers fusion dishes and a lively weekend atmosphere. Try Nordic-style tacos or enjoy perfectly mixed cocktails. Main: NKr 145. Closed Sun. & Mon. Visit wamazoniabybar.no.

Gamle Rådhus

Housed in Oslo's first town hall, this Norwegian restaurant offers traditional fish and game dishes. Located at Nedre Slottsgt. 1, Sentrum. Main: NKr 320. Closed Sun. Call P22-42-01-07 or visit gamleraadhus.no.

Lofoten Fiskerestaurant

Located at Stranden 75, Aker Brygge, Lofoten offers fresh seafood and harbor views. Main: NKr 350. Call P22-83-08-08 or visit lofoten-fiskerestaurant.no.

Olivia Aker Brygge

This family-friendly Italian restaurant at Stranden 3 offers wood-fired pizzas with harbor views. Main: NKr 180. Call P23-11-54-70 or visit oliviarestauranter.no.

Olivia Tjuvholmen

A family favorite at Bryggegangen, serving pizzas and pastas with a buzzing atmosphere. Main: NKr 180. Call P23-11-54-70 or visit oliviarestauranter.no.

Solsiden
Located at Akershusstranda, Aker Brygge, Solsiden offers a sunny ambiance and decadent desserts. Main: NKr 330. Call P22-33-36-30 or visit solsiden.no.

Statholdergaarden
This award-winning restaurant at Rådhusgate 11 offers Norwegian delicacies with a fine dining setting. Main: NKr 470. Closed Sun. Call P22-41-88-00 or visit statholdergaarden.no.

Vippa
At Akershusstranda 2, Sentrum, Vippa is a vibrant cultural hub with diverse food options. Main: NKr 150. Closed Mon. Visit vippa.no.

Hotels

First Hotel Grims Grenka
Located at 5 Kvadraturen, this design hotel offers modern rooms and central location. Rooms from NKr 1196. Free breakfast. Call P23-10-72-00 or visit firsthotels.com.

The Thief
Located at Landgangen 1, Tjuvholmen, this boutique hotel offers luxury and free museum admission. Rooms from NKr 3000. Free pool and breakfast. Call P24-00-40-00 or visit thethief.com.

Nightlife

BA3 BARS
Located at Bygdøy Allé 3, Frogner, BA3 features four bars catering to different moods. Call P22-55-11-86 or visit ba3.no.

Shopping Centers

Aker Brygge Shopping
At Støperigata 2, Aker Brygge, this waterfront shopping center features over 30 boutiques and bars. Call P22-83-26-80 or visit akerbrygge.no.

Activities

SAILING

The Christian Radich, located at Akershusstranda 9, Kvadraturen, is a tall ship with striking white sails and towering masts. It offers a variety of sailing trips, including multi-day tours along Norway's coast. No sailing experience is necessary, but passengers should be prepared for rough seas and high waves, as well as participating in crew duties. Prices and specific details can be found on radich.no.

Red Cottage by the lake, Norway

Frogner

Oslo West, which includes Frogner and Majorstuen, combines classic Scandinavian elegance with modern European flair. Here, hip boutiques, top-tier restaurants, and prestigious galleries sit alongside embassies and ambassadorial residences. This vibrant area surrounds Bygdøy Allé, making it a bustling district rich in culture and style.

Getting Around

The area is well-connected with frequent tram and bus routes that easily take you to the Sentrum. While the subway does not pass directly through this neighborhood, its proximity allows for convenient access to other parts of the city.

Attractions

Internasjonale Barnekunstmuseet (International Museum of Children's Art)

The International Museum of Children's Art, established by Russian immigrant Rafael Goldin, features a unique collection of children's artwork from over 150 countries. This museum offers an insight into the world through the eyes of children, showcasing textiles, paintings, and other art forms. It is located at Lille Frøens vei 4, Majorstuen. Admission is 75 NOK, and it is open from Tuesday to Friday. The museum is closed from mid-August to mid-September and on Mondays. For more information, visit www.barnekunst.no or call 22-46-85-73.

Nationalbibliotek (National Library)

The National Library in Oslo boasts grand facades, classical statues, and painted dome ceilings. It holds the complete cultural and knowledge heritage of Norway, offering a vast collection primarily in Norwegian. The library hosts regular exhibits, concerts, lectures, and guided tours (call ahead for English-language services). A café inside serves sandwiches and pastries throughout the day. The library is located at Henrik Ibsens gt. 110, Frogner, and is open daily, except Mondays. Visit www.nb.no or call 81-00-13-00 for more details.

Oslo Bymuseum (Oslo City Museum)

The Oslo City Museum, located at Frognerveien 67, offers a two-floor exhibit that takes visitors through Oslo's transformation from its prominence in 1050 to the urban developments of the 20th century. Notable relics include the red coats of the first Oslo police officers from the 1700s and the town's first fire wagon. Admission is 90 NOK, and the museum is open Tuesday to Sunday, with Mondays closed. For more details, visit www.oslomuseum.no or call 23-28-41-70.

Skøytemuseet (Ice Skating Museum)

Nestled in Frogner Stadium, the Ice Skating Museum celebrates Norway's rich history in ice skating. The museum showcases trophies, Olympic medals, and displays of various skates, from ancient bone skates to modern versions. Photographs of skating legends such as Johann Olav Koss and Hjalmar Andersen line the walls. The museum is open Wednesday to Saturday, from 10:00 AM to 3:00 PM, and closed on Mondays. For more information, visit www.skoytemuseet.no or call 22-43-49-20.

Vigelandsmuseet (Vigeland Museum)

The Vigeland Museum is housed in the former studio and residence of Norwegian sculptor Gustav Vigeland. It displays models of almost all his works, along with sculptures, drawings, woodcuts, and the original plans for Vigeland Park. The museum is located at Nobelsgt. 32, Frogner. Admission is free, but the museum is closed on Mondays. For further details, visit www.vigeland.museum.no or call 23-49-37-00.

Vigelandsparken (Vigeland Sculpture Park)

Vigeland Sculpture Park, one of Oslo's favorite parks, is home to 212 bronze, granite, and wrought-iron sculptures by Gustav Vigeland. Highlights include the towering granite Monolith, featuring 121 nude figures, and the popular Angry Boy sculpture. The park also includes a museum for those wishing to explore more of Vigeland's work. The park is located in Frogner and is open year-round, with free admission. Visit www.vigeland.museum.no for more information.

Restaurants

Á L'aise

A fine French restaurant offering a luxurious, candlelit atmosphere. Expect a wine trolley, cheese selection, and five-star service. Average main: NKr500. Majorstuen, Frogner, 6 Sun-Mon. www.alaise.no, +47 21 05 57 00.

Bølgen & Moi Gimle
Minimalist and family-friendly, this eatery serves hearty breakfasts and an extensive wine list. Average main: NKr255. Bygdøy Allé 53, Frogner. www.bolgenogmoi.no, +47 24 11 53 00.

Feinschmecker
Fusion dining with a global twist, elegant dining, and an interesting wine list. Average main: NKr400. Balchensgt. 5, Frogner. Closed Sun. www.feinschmecker.no, +47 22 12 93 80.

FYR
Nordic fare served in a cozy, candlelit bistro with a terrace. Known for generous portions and affordable bar menus. Average main: NKr350. Underhaugsveien 28, Majorstuen. www.fyrbistronomi.no, +47 459 16 392.

Hos Thea
Scandinavian cuisine served in an intimate setting with French and Spanish influences. Average main: NKr320. Gabelsgt. 11, Frogner. www.hosthea.no, +47 22 44 68 74.

Kolonihagen Frogner
A cozy, botanical eatery offering vegan-friendly Nordic comfort food. Average main: NKr295. Frognerveien 33, Frogner. Closed Sun-Mon. kolonihagenfrogner.no, +47 993 16 810.

L'Ardoise
A neighborhood brasserie serving refined meals and a legendary dessert menu. Average main: NKr525. Theresegt. 20B, Frogner. Closed Sun-Mon. www.lardoise.no, +47 22 11 09 65.

Olivia Hegdehaugsveien
An Italian eatery offering Roman-style dishes in a cozy, family-friendly setting. Average main: NKr200. Hegdehaugsveien, Majorstuen. oliviarestauranter.no, +47 23 11 54 70.

Palace Grill
French fusion cuisine in a stylish, intimate restaurant near the Royal Palace. Average main: NKr300. Solligaten 2, Frogner. www.palacegrill.no, +47 23 11 40 00.

Pizza da Mimmo
Oslo's best pizzeria, known for made-to-order thin-crust pizzas. Average main: NKr180. Behrensgt. 2, Frogner. www.pizzadamimmo.no, +47 22 40 20 00. No lunch.

Village Tandoori
A charming Indian spot with antique decor and authentic tandoori chicken. Average main: NKr220. Bygdøy Allé 65, Frogner. villagetandoori.no, +47 22 56 10 25.

Hotels

Clarion Collection Hotel Gabelshus
Chic boutique hotel offering a complimentary evening meal and convenient location. Rooms from: NKr1200. Gabelsgt. 23, Frogner. www.choicehotels.com, +47 23 27 65 00.

Cochs Pensjonat
Affordable B&B with a central location near the Royal Palace and shopping. Rooms from: NKr500. Parkvn. 25, Majorstuen. www.cochspensjonat.no, +47 23 33 24 00. No meals.

Guldsmeden Hotel
Inviting hotel with a cozy reception area and on-site hammam. Rooms from: NKr1300. Parkveien 78, Frogner. guldsmedenhotels.com, +47 23 27 40 00.

Sommerro
A modern hotel offering a rooftop pool and in-house theater. Rooms from: NKr1490. Sommerrogata 1, Frogner. sommerrohouse.com, +47 56 78 90 00.

Villa Frogner
Elegant B&B with traditional decor and homemade breakfasts. Rooms from: NKr700. Nordraaksgt. 26, Frogner. www.villafrogner.no, +47 22 56 07 42. Free breakfast.

Nightlife

Gathering Places
A colorful venue with bars on each floor and live performances. Bygdøy Allé 3, Frogner. www.ba3.no, +47 22 55 11 86. Closed Sun-Mon.

Champagneria
Classy wine bar with tapas and sidewalk seating in Frogner. Frognerveien 2, Frogner. +47 21 08 09 09.

Josefine Inn
A 19th-century villa serving aperitifs and digestifs in a charming setting. Josefinesgt. 16, Majorstuen. +47 22 69 34 99. www.josefine.no.

Shopping

Børresen Homannsbyen Antikk og Brukt
A vast antique store filled with treasures and shipping options. Hegdehaugsveien 36, Frogner. +47 22 60 69 69.

Damms Antikvariat
An antiquarian bookstore with rare manuscripts, books, and maps. Frederik Stangsgt. 41, Frogner. www.damms.no, +47 22 60 69 69. Closed Sun.

Gabel Antikviteter
A shop offering fascinating tableware, porcelain, and more. Bygdøy allé 33, Frogner. +47 918 43 123. www.gabel.no.

Galleri Gimle
Specializing in 18th-century furniture and chandeliers. Gimleveien 21, Frogner. +47 92 86 35 95.

Holmenkollen

Holmenkollen, a prominent hill visible from various parts of Oslo, is home to the famous ski jump and a network of ski trails, offering stunning views of the city. Over the years, more accommodation and dining options have been added, making it an even more popular destination. The area is easily accessible by Metro, with Line 1 heading directly to the Holmenkollen ski jump. Trams and buses also provide quick connections to Sentrum, taking around 20-30 minutes. Additionally, Tryvann and Frognerseteren serve as excellent starting points for hiking throughout the year.

Attractions

Emanuel Vigeland Museum
This museum, though not as famous as its sibling Gustav Vigeland's creations, showcases the work of Emanuel Vigeland. The artist's provocative frescoes, often exploring themes of sexuality and nature, have earned the museum a reputation for being bold and captivating. Located slightly off the beaten path in the residential area of Slemdal, this museum is worth the visit. To get here, take Metro Line 1 from Nationaltheatret Station towards Frognerseteren and disembark at Slemdal. The museum is open Monday to Saturday but is closed on Sundays and has limited hours from mid-May to mid-September. You can find more details on their official website at www.emanuelvigeland.museum.no. Address: Emanuel Vigeland Museum, Grimelundsvn. 22-14-57-88, Oslo. Admission fees may vary depending on the time of year.

Frognerseteren Scenic Drive
Frognerseteren is an essential destination for both locals and visitors seeking panoramic views of Oslo and the fjords. This scenic spot is popular for cross-country skiing in winter and traditional Sunday hikes. Frognerseteren features two restaurants housed in a building dating back to 1891. The self-service Kafe Seterstua offers sandwiches and waffles, while Restaurant Finstua specializes in Norwegian smoked and salted dishes. The building's rustic log design evokes traditional Norwegian mountain life, offering a peaceful retreat just a short distance from the city center. The address for Frognerseteren is Holmenkollen, Frognerseteren, Oslo. For more details, visit www.frognerseteren.no.

Holmenkollen Ski Museum

The Holmenkollen Ski Museum, part of the iconic Holmenkollen Ski Jump, provides visitors with a deep dive into 4,000 years of ski history. Opened in 1892 and continuously renovated, the ski jump remains a prominent feature of Oslo's skyline and hosts international ski events. Visitors can experience a ski-jump simulator that gives them the feel of a professional jumper. The museum is located at Kongevn. 5, Holmenkollen, Oslo. Admission fees are NOK 140, and guided tours are available. For more information, visit holmenkollen.com or call +47 22 92 32 00. The museum is part of Oslo's skiing legacy and offers an immersive experience for families and ski enthusiasts alike.

Restaurants

De Fem Stuer

Located in Scandic Holmenkollen Park Hotel, De Fem Stuer serves modern Nordic and international cuisine with views over Oslo. Average main: NOK 350. Address: Holmenkollen Park Hotel, Kongevn. 26, Holmenkollen. Website: www.scandichotels.com. Phone: +47 22 92 20 00.

Finstua

Finstua offers traditional Norwegian fare with stunning mountain views above Holmenkollen. Average main: NOK 385. Address: Holmenkollen 200, Holmenkollen. Website: www.frognerseteren.no. Phone: +47 22 92 40 40.

Hotels

Scandic Holmenkollen Park

This hotel, dating back to 1894, offers unparalleled views of Oslo from a mountaintop location. Prices from: NOK 900. Address: Kongevn. 26, Holmenkollen. Website: holmenkollenparkhotel.no. Phone: +47 22 92 20 00.

Oslo Vinterpark (Oslo Winter Park)

Oslo Winter Park, located in Holmenkollen, features 11 slopes, six lifts, and a terrain park. The ski season runs from late November to April. Address: Tryvannsveien 64, Holmenkollen. Website: www.oslovinterpark.no. Phone: +47 22 14 36 10.

Activities

Oslo Winter Park (Oslo Vinterpark)

Oslo Winter Park, located in Holmenkollen, offers 11 downhill slopes, six lifts, and a terrain park with a half-pipe for snowboarders. The park is open from late November to April, with night skiing available on weekends. Address: Tryvannsveien 64, Holmenkollen. Phone: +47 22 14 36 10. Website: www.oslovinterpark.no.

Damstredet & telthusbakken oslo norway

Rodeløkka in Oslo, the wooden village of Norway

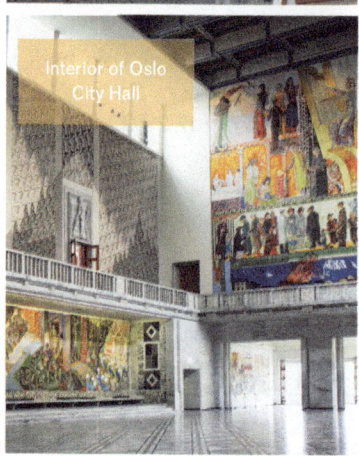

Interior of Oslo City Hall

Hiking in Norway

Page 52

- Bygdøy
- Sentrum
- Grünerløkka
- Aker Brygge
- Frogner
- Holmenkollen

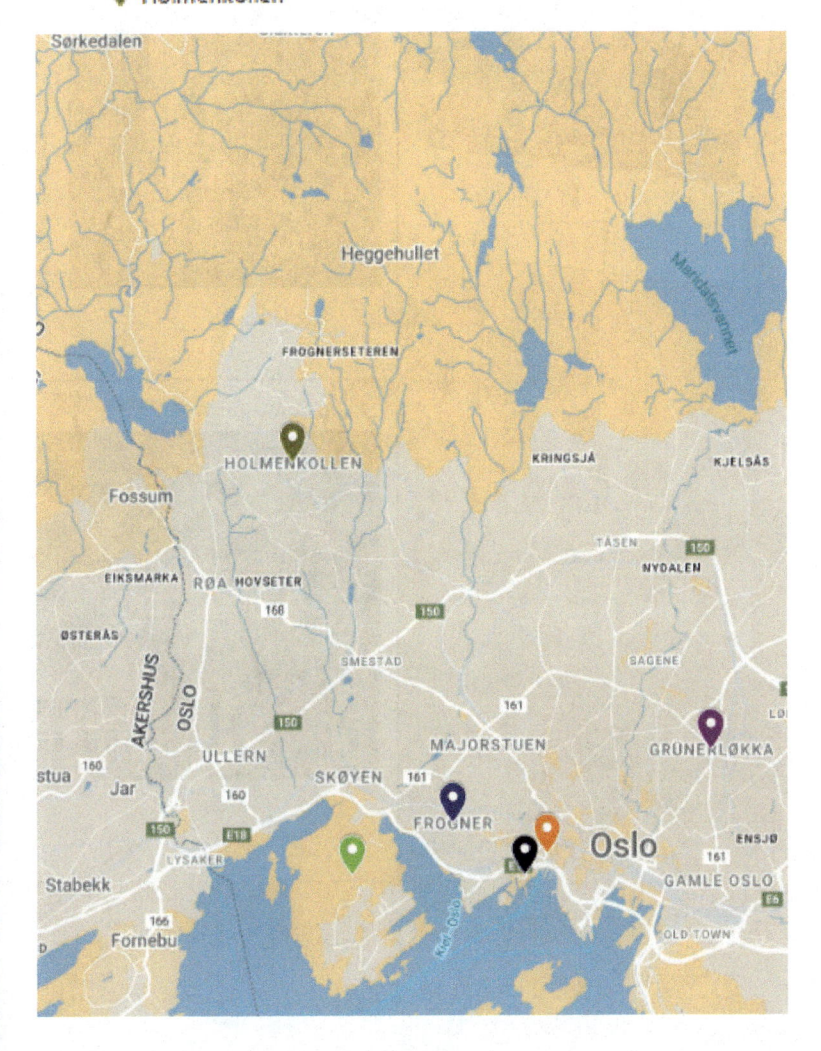

CHAPTER 3

BERGEN

Bergen, Norway's second-largest city, captivates visitors with its vibrant blend of nature and history. Surrounded by lush mountains and sparkling fjords, the city boasts picturesque scenes of colorful wooden houses, cobblestone streets, and historic Hanseatic structures. Known as "Trebyen" (Wooden City), "Regnbyen" (Rainy City), and "Fjordbyen" (Gateway to the Fjords), Bergen offers a unique charm.

The city's residents embrace the outdoors, enjoying activities like hiking, biking, fishing, and boating. Whether it's taking the funicular to nearby mountains or spending time at their fjordside cabins, locals are deeply connected to the natural beauty around them. While rain is frequent—averaging 260 days a year—visitors quickly adapt, equipped with rain jackets and umbrellas.

Bergen has a rich cultural legacy, with figures like composer Edvard Grieg and violinist Ole Bull leaving lasting marks on Norwegian arts. Today, Bergen continues to foster creativity, with renowned residents like pianist Leif Ove Andsnes and author Gunnar Staalesen contributing to the city's vibrant artistic scene. The city also hosts a variety of festivals that attract national and international talent.

Best Time to Visit Bergen

The best time to visit Bergen is from May to September when the weather is relatively mild. Temperatures rarely exceed 80°F, though sudden showers are common, so carrying a jacket is advised. Autumn also offers pleasant weather with crisp nights and stunning fall foliage, especially on Mt. Fløyen. Winters, though cold and rarely snowy, offer the opportunity to explore ski resorts just 90 minutes from the city.

Planning Your Visit

Bergen is a compact city, but to fully appreciate its attractions, plan for a few days of exploration. Spend one day discovering Bryggen's UNESCO-listed buildings and its fortress, and another in Sentrum, where a cluster of museums awaits. If you're interested in the historical homes of Edvard Grieg and Ole Bull, a half-day trip is recommended.

If visiting outside summer, keep in mind that daylight hours are shorter. Museums also close earlier during winter, so prioritize your visits to the most important sites, such as Bergenhus Festning, which shuts earlier in colder months despite having outdoor areas open year-round.

Getting to and Around Bergen

Flights to Bergen are available from major airlines like SAS, Norwegian, and Widerøe, as well as international carriers like British Airways, KLM, and Lufthansa. Flesland Airport, located 30 minutes from the city, is easily accessible by Flybussen, which departs every 15 minutes and costs around NKr 139. Taxis are also available at the airport, with fares ranging from NKr 450 to NKr 550 to the city center. Alternatively, the light rail offers a more economical option, taking about 45 minutes to the downtown area for NKr 40.

Transportation Options in Bergen

Flybussen (Airport Bus)
Flybussen provides a quick and efficient way to get from Bergen Airport to the city center. The airport bus departs every 15 minutes, with the trip taking around 30 minutes and costing approximately NKr 139. The service operates from the airport to downtown Bergen. For more details, visit Flybussen.

Boat and Ferry Services
Bergen's boat services are a vital part of its transport network. The Kystruten coastal express, run by Hurtigruten and Havila, departs daily on an 11-day round trip to Kirkenes in northern Norway. Other services include fjord cruises from Rødne Fjord Cruise, Norled, and Fjord Line, all offering scenic routes to various fjords and popular destinations like Flåm and Stavanger. Cruises depart from Skoltegrunnskaien and Jekteviken/Dokkeskjærskaien, both within walking distance of downtown. For schedules, visit Fjord Line, Hurtigruten,

Norled, and Havila Voyages.

Bus Services

Nor-Way Bussekspress operates multiple daily buses between Bergen and Oslo, with the journey taking about 9 to 10 hours. Skyss is the primary bus operator within Bergen, offering both daytime and night services, including late-night buses on weekends. For bus schedules and information, visit Nor-Way Bussekspress and Skyss.

Driving to Bergen

Bergen is 462 km from Oslo, accessible by three main routes. The scenic Route 7 passes through the Hardangervidda Plateau, while other routes, like the E16 and Route 52, take you through tunnels, including the world's longest, the Lærdalstunnelen. Be aware that mountain passes may close in winter. For up-to-date road conditions, check Statens Vegvesen.

Taxi Services

Taxis in Bergen are readily available from various stands around the city, with Bergen Taxi being the largest service provider. You can also book a taxi in advance through their central office. For taxi bookings and details, visit Bergen Taxi.

Train Service to Bergen

Vy operates the scenic train route between Oslo and Bergen, one of the world's most beautiful train rides. The journey takes around seven hours, with prices starting from NKr 249 if booked early. The train station in Bergen is centrally located, within walking distance of many hotels. For more details, visit Vy.

Dining Scene in Bergen

Bergen boasts an impressive dining scene, with numerous restaurants earning international recognition. Being a coastal city, seafood is a key feature in most menus, with traditional dishes frequently served alongside innovative takes on New Nordic cuisine. Many local restaurants pride themselves on using seasonal, locally sourced ingredients, often sourced directly from specific farmers or ranchers. Two standout establishments, Lysverket and Bare, have earned Michelin stars, further cementing the city's culinary reputation.

Festivals and Cultural Events

Bergen International Festival
This prominent cultural event takes place annually at the end of May and into early June. The festival celebrates classical music, jazz, ballet, theater, and the arts, drawing well-known artists from around the world. The festival brings an exciting blend of music and performances to the city, making it a must-visit for art lovers. More information can be found on their official website Bergen International Festival.

Bergenfest
Held each June, Bergenfest is a three-day outdoor music festival hosted at Bergenhus Festning. The event features a mix of international stars and local bands, creating an energetic atmosphere against the historic backdrop of the fortress. For full event details, visit Bergenfest.

Visitor Information

Tourist Information
For all your travel queries in Bergen, Visit Bergen is your go-to resource. Located at Strandkaien 3 in the city center, the office provides maps, guides, and useful tips for exploring Bergen. You can reach them at +47 55 20 00 or visit their website at Visit Bergen.

Bergen old town aerial view

Bryggen

Bergen, founded in 1070 by Olav Kyrre, began as a commercial hub and evolved into a key trading center under Hanseatic merchants in the 14th century. The iconic Hanseatic wooden buildings on Bryggen, painted in vivid hues of red, blue, yellow, and green, are now UNESCO World Heritage sites. These structures house shops, restaurants, and museums and glow beautifully when illuminated at night. Together with the Rosenkrantz Tower, Fløyen, and moored yachts, they create a breathtaking reflection on the harbor waters, offering one of northern Europe's most picturesque cityscapes. South of Bryggen, Vågsbunnen stands out as a lively neighborhood filled with trendy bars, clubs, and designer boutiques.

Attractions

Bergen Domkirke (Bergen Cathedral)
Bergen Cathedral's eclectic architecture reflects its long and turbulent history, with the Gothic-style choir and lower towers dating back to the 13th century. A cannonball embedded in the tower wall commemorates a 1665 battle between English and Dutch ships. Regular organ concerts enhance the experience of visiting this historic site. Located on Domkirke Street, it is accessible through Bryggen at +47 59-32-73.

Bergenhus Festning (Bergenhus Fortress)
The Bergenhus Fortress features two main attractions: Håkonshallen and Rosenkrantztårnet. Håkonshallen, built in the 1200s as a royal ceremonial hall under King Håkon Håkonsson, was restored after damage from a 1944 explosion. Rosenkrantztårnet, constructed in the 1560s, served as a fortified residence. Both sites are open to visitors, although Håkonshallen may close for events or holidays. Visit Bryggen and explore these landmarks with information available at www.bymuseet.no/en or by contacting +47 55-30-80-30.

Bryggen (Bryggen Hanseatic Wharf)
Bryggen, a UNESCO World Heritage site since 1979, is an unmissable attraction. The reconstructed 14th-century wooden buildings along the harbor feature boutiques, restaurants, and charming wooden alleys. Despite surviving multiple fires, including one in 1955, the area retains its historic charm, making it a delightful spot to explore on sunny days.

Bryggens Museum

The Bryggens Museum showcases archaeological finds from Bergen's medieval period. Highlights include a 1300s exhibit featuring reconstructed living quarters, tools, and shoes from the city's heyday as Norway's largest and most cosmopolitan trading center. Located at Dreggsallmenningen 3, the museum charges NKr 100 for entry. Visit www.bymuseet.no/en for details or call +47 55-30-80-30.

Det Hanseatiske Museum og Schøtstuene (The Hanseatic Museum and Schøtstuene)

The Hanseatic Museum, housed in a 16th-century building, offers a glimpse into the life of German merchants and their apprentices. The snug, boxed-in beds upstairs provided warmth in the unheated structure. Guided tours are available in Norwegian, German, French, and English during summer. Visit Finnegården in Bryggen or call +47 53-00-61-10. For more information, see www.museumvest.no/english.

Fisketorget (Bergen Fish Market)

Bergen Fish Market, located at Torget 5, combines modern architecture with traditional open-air market vibes. Here, visitors can savor seafood lunches of shrimp or salmon baguettes while enjoying views of the harbor. The market also offers fruits, vegetables, flowers, and local crafts. Contact +47 55-55-20-00 or visit Bryggen for details.

Fløibanen (Mount Fløyen Funicular)

A ride on the Fløibanen funicular provides stunning views of Bergen from Mount Fløyen, 320 meters above sea level. The eight-minute journey operates every half hour and leads to a summit with a restaurant, café, shop, and playground. Tickets cost NKr 65 each way. For more, visit Vetrlidsalmenningen 21 or www.floyen.no/en, or call +47 55-33-68-00.

Lille Øvregaten

This quaint cobblestone lane, meaning "Little Upper Street," showcases Bergen's charm with its 19th-century clapboard houses. Lille Øvregaten offers a nostalgic glimpse of the city from a century ago, perfect for a peaceful stroll.

Mariakirken (St. Mary's Church)

Dating to 1170, Mariakirken is Bergen's oldest building still in use. Its twin spires, intricate 15th-century altarpiece, ornate pulpit, and biblical wall paintings are noteworthy. Located at Dreggen 15, the church charges NKr 75 for entry mid-September to mid-May, while it is free from mid-May to mid-September. It is closed on weekends and certain days in other months. Visit kirken.no/nb-NO or call +47 55-59-71-75 for details.

Restaurants

Bare
Bare offers a refined dining experience with 7- or 11-course menus showcasing innovative Norwegian cuisine. Located at 2 Vågsbunnen, meals start at NKr1250. Closed Sun. and Mon., with no lunch service. Visit barerestaurant.no or call 400-02-455.

Bryggeloftet & Stuene
This cozy eatery serves hearty Norwegian dishes like reindeer fillet and fish soup amidst maritime-themed decor. Located at 11 Bryggen, mains average NKr350. Visit bryggeloftet.no or call 55-30-20-70.

Bryggeriet
Located at Torget 2, Bryggeriet brews its own beer, complemented by fresh seafood and fjord views. Mains average NKr250; closed Mon. and Tues. Visit bryggeriet.biz or call 55-55-31-55.

Enhjørningen
This seafood restaurant in a historic Bryggen building serves fresh dishes like steamed halibut. Meals average NKr360, and it is closed Sun. and Sept.-mid-May. Visit enhjorningen.no or call 55-30-69-50.

Fish Me
Located in the fish market at Strandkaien 3, this spot offers fresh seafood and sushi with views of Bryggen. Mains average NKr250. Visit fishme.no or call 450-23-000.

Nama

Nama, at Lodin Lepps gt. 2B, offers Japanese dishes like sushi and robatayaki in a chic setting. Mains average NKr275. Visit namasushi.no or call 55-32-20-10.

Restaurant 1877

This nostalgic venue in Kjøttbasaren emphasizes local ingredients in dishes averaging NKr795. Closed Sun., it's at 2 Vetrlidsallmenningen. Visit restaurant1877.no or call 928-71-877.

Soya Restaurant

Soya blends authentic Chinese cuisine with Scandinavian design at 6 Bryggen. Mains average NKr279. Visit soyarestaurant.no or call 56-90-12-55.

Taperia Tapas & Pinxos

Located at Skostredet 1b, this spot serves authentic Spanish tapas in a cozy two-floor space. Mains average NKr250. Visit taperia.no.

To Kokker

To Kokker offers traditional Norwegian cuisine with a modern twist in a 300-year-old Bryggen building. Mains average NKr595; closed Sun. Visit tokokker.no or call 55-30-69-55.

26 North

26 North at Bryggen 47 specializes in New Nordic dishes under a stunning glass ceiling. Mains average NKr325; no dinner service Fri. or Sat. Visit 26north.no/bergen or call 477-10-467.

Villani

Villani serves wood-fired pizzas and homemade pasta at Skostredet 9a. Mains average NKr259. Visit villani.no or call 55-31-55-55.

Bare

Bare offers a refined dining experience with 7- or 11-course menus showcasing innovative Norwegian cuisine. Located at 2 Vågsbunnen, meals start at NKr1250. Closed Sun. and Mon., with no lunch service. Visit barerestaurant.no or call 400-02-455.

Bryggeloftet & Stuene
This cozy eatery serves hearty Norwegian dishes like reindeer fillet and fish soup amidst maritime-themed decor. Located at 11 Bryggen, mains average NKr350. Visit bryggeloftet.no or call 55-30-20-70.

Bryggeriet
Located at Torget 2, Bryggeriet brews its own beer, complemented by fresh seafood and fjord views. Mains average NKr250; closed Mon. and Tues. Visit bryggeriet.biz or call 55-55-31-55.

Enhjørningen
This seafood restaurant in a historic Bryggen building serves fresh dishes like steamed halibut. Meals average NKr360, and it is closed Sun. and Sept.-mid-May. Visit enhjorningen.no or call 55-30-69-50.

Nightlife

Baklommen Bar
This cozy cocktail spot at Enhjørningsgården 29, Bryggen features unique wooden beams and a charming ambiance. Closed on Sundays, it serves crafted cocktails in a historic setting. Visit tokokker.no/baklommen-bar or call 55-32-27-47 for details.

Bar 3
Bar 3, at Rosenkrantzgt. 3, Bryggen, offers games like shuffleboard and Ping-Pong alongside craft beers in a relaxed space. Contact 488-89-200 or visit bar3.no. Closed Sundays.

Biblioteket Bar
Located at Vetrlidsallmenningen 2, Bryggen, this elegant cocktail lounge overlooks the harbor, hosting live music and DJs at a conversational volume. Closed Sundays; find more at facebook.com/BiblioteketBar or call 55-01-18-85.

Folk & Røvere
Serving a wide range of craft beers, this casual bar at Vågsbunnen 4 features sidewalk seating and a covered patio. Visit folkogrovere.net or call 57-00-14-99.

No Stress
This nostalgic cocktail bar at Hollendergaten 11, Vågsbunnen, combines retro furnishings with creative drinks. Learn more at nostressbar.no.

Performing Arts

Litteraturhuset
Litteraturhuset at Østre Skostredet 5-7 hosts book readings, debates, and a café. Visit litthusbergen.no for schedules. Closed Sundays and Mondays.

Shopping

Berle Bryggen
Located at Bryggen 5, this shop offers Dale of Norway sweaters, pewter crafts, and souvenirs. Closed Sundays; visit berlebryggen.com.

Oleana
The flagship store at Strandkaien 2A features Norwegian-designed textiles and clothing. Closed Sundays; see oleana.no for more.

Råvarene
Råvarene, at Marken 9, promotes sustainable, waste-free products. Closed Sundays; details at raavarene.com.

Ting Bergen
Find stylish gifts and designer items at Ting Bergen, Bryggen 13. Visit ting.no or call 55-21-54-80.

Sentrum

While many visitors gravitate toward Bryggen, Sentrum serves as Bergen's vibrant core. Encircling the scenic Lake Lille Lungegårdsvann are the KODE museums, showcasing some of the city's finest art collections. Byparken offers a serene space for leisurely walks or sunbathing during summer, creating a peaceful escape amidst the urban setting. In the evening, Ole Bulls plass becomes lively with its array of cafés and restaurants, culminating at the Norwegian Theater.

Navigating Sentrum

Bergen's compact city center is ideal for exploring on foot, with most attractions accessible within a short walk. Both the train and bus stations are conveniently close to Sentrum, making it easy to arrive and move around.

Attractions

Grieghallen
Grieghallen, a striking glass-and-concrete performance venue in Edvard Griegs plass 1, Sentrum, is the home of the Bergen Philharmonic Orchestra and hosts the Bergen International Festival. Built in 1978 and named after composer Edvard Grieg (1843-1907), its exceptional acoustics make it a premier destination for cultural events year-round. Visit grieghallen.no for details.

KODE 1

This Neoclassical building, originally called Permanenten, opened in 1896 and overlooks the picturesque Byparken. It showcases the Sølvskatten (Silver Treasure), a glittering collection of gold, silver, and metalworks, alongside European and Asian antiques. Located at Nordahl Bruns gate 9, Sentrum, admission costs NKr 150, including a two-day pass to all KODE museums. Closed on Mondays. More at kodebergen.no/en/find-us/kode-1.

KODE 2

The most modern museum in the KODE complex, KODE 2, features rotating art exhibits and a well-stocked bookstore with works on art, architecture, and design. Its Café Smakverket provides a casual dining experience. Located at Rasmus Meyers allé 3, Sentrum, admission is NKr 150 for a two-day pass to all KODE museums. Closed on Mondays. Visit kodebergen.no/en/find-us/kode-2.

KODE 3

Dedicated to Norwegian art, KODE 3 houses masterpieces by Edvard Munch, J.C. Dahl, and other renowned artists. Designed by Ole Landmark in 1916, it was initially built to display Rasmus Meyer's private collection. Located at Rasmus Meyers allé 7, Sentrum, admission is NKr 150, valid for two days across all KODE museums. Closed on Mondays. For information, visit kodebergen.no/en/find-us/kode-3.

KODE 4

Resembling a giant battery, KODE 4 offers a journey through art history, displaying works from the 13th to the 20th century, including pieces by Pablo Picasso and Nikolai Astrup. KunstLab, on the ground floor, caters to children, while Lysverket restaurant serves Michelin-starred seafood. Located at Rasmus Meyers allé 9, Sentrum, admission is NKr 150 for a two-day pass to all KODE museums. Closed on Mondays. Details at kodebergen.no/en/find-us/kode-4.

Lepramuseet (The Leprosy Museum)

St. George's Hospital, once a sanctuary for leprosy patients over 500 years, is now a museum honoring those affected and Norway's contributions to leprosy research. Highlights include the chapel's hand-carved woodwork and small examining rooms. Located at Kong Oscars gate 59, Sentrum, admission is NKr 120, open early May to September. Closed from September to mid-May. Visit bymuseet.no/museum/lepramuseet/ or call 55-30-80-37.

Musikkpaviljongen
Constructed in 1888, this Moorish-inspired cast-iron bandstand graces the serene Byparken. It serves as a historical landmark and a peaceful retreat amidst the city bustle. Find it at Olav Kyrres gate 27, Sentrum.

Restaurants

Colonialen 44
Colonialen 44 offers a refined four-course tasting menu blending Norwegian and international culinary techniques. Located at Kong Oscars gate 44, Sentrum. For reservations, call 55901600 or visit colonialen.no/44. Average main course is NKr550.

Kulturhuset
Kulturhuset emphasizes sustainable dining with vegetarian, vegan, and meat dishes. Find it at Vaskerelven 8, Downtown; the average main costs NKr185. Check their menu at kulturhusetibergen.no.

Lysverket
Located in KODE 4, Lysverket features a 10-course tasting menu highlighting seasonal, local ingredients. At Rasmus Meyers allé 9, Sentrum. Visit lysverket.no or call 55603100; the average meal costs NKr1849.

Marg & Bein
Marg & Bein celebrates traditional Norwegian cuisine. Located at Fosswinckels gate 18, Sentrum. Average main course is NKr289. Visit marg-bein.no or call 55323234.

MM Café og Bar
Located at Olav Vs plass 4, Sentrum, MM Café offers globally inspired dishes using local ingredients. Average main is NKr199. Call 46838034 or visit mmbergen.no for details.

Pingvinen
Pingvinen serves hearty Norwegian meals at Vaskerelven 14, Sentrum. The average main costs NKr180. For more, visit pingvinen.no or call 55604646.

Wesselstuen
Wesselstuen specializes in Norwegian fare like reindeer steak in an atmospheric 18th-century setting. Located at Øvre Ole Bulls plass 6, Sentrum, with mains averaging NKr250. Call 55554949 or visit wesselstuen.no.

Coffee and Quick Bites

Café Opera
Café Opera offers fish soup and pan-fried salmon at Engen 18, Sentrum. Average main is NKr175. Call 55230315 or visit cafeopera.org.

Hotels

Citybox Bergen
Citybox provides simple, budget-friendly rooms at Nygårdsgate 31, Sentrum, starting at NKr699. Visit citybox.no/bergen-en or call 55312500.

Hotel Norge by Scandic
This upscale hotel at Bulls plass, Sentrum, offers rooms starting at NKr2045. Visit scandichotels.no or call 55552100.

Hotel Oleana
Hotel Oleana features stylish accommodations at Øvre Ole Bulls plass 5, Sentrum, starting at NKr1500. Call 55554000 or visit hoteloleana.com.

Hotel Zander K
Located at Zander Kaaes gate 8, Sentrum, rooms at Zander K start at NKr1192. Visit zanderk.no or call 55362040.

Scandic Byparken
Located at Christies gate 5-7, Sentrum, Scandic Byparken offers rooms from NKr1418. Visit scandichotels.com or call 55545600.

Thon Hotel Bristol
Thon Hotel Bristol provides charming accommodations at Torgallmenningen 11, Sentrum, starting at NKr1552. Visit thonhotels.no or call 55551000.

Nightlife

Fincken
Fincken, Bergen's gay bar, is at Nygårdsgaten 2A, Sentrum, closed Sunday to Tuesday. Call 55321316 or visit fincken.no.

JADA Roofgarden
JADA Roofgarden offers drinks on a rooftop terrace at Småstrandgaten 3, Bergen. Call 45837475 or visit jadaroofgarden.no.

Kava Roofgarden
Kava features stylish bars and fjord views at Strandgaten 15, Bergen. Visit kavaroofgarden.no for details.

LouLou
LouLou, located in Hotel Norge by Scandic, offers cocktails and a futuristic dance floor. Visit loulou.no for details.

Storm Bar
Storm Bar is ideal for pre-theater drinks at Øvre Ole Bulls plass 3, Bergen. Visit olebullhuset.no/bar for more information.

Shopping

Bergen Storsenter
This shopping center near the bus terminal features diverse stores at Strømgate 8, Sentrum. Visit bergenstorsenter.no.

Galleriet
Galleriet, with 70+ shops, is located at Torgallmenningen 8, Sentrum. Visit galleriet.com for details.

Hjertholm
Hjertholm sells Scandinavian crafts at Torgallmenningen 8, Sentrum. Visit hjertholm.no.

Høyer
Høyer offers luxury fashion at Torgallmenningen 2, Downtown. Visit hoyer.no for details.

Kløverhuset

Kløverhuset, Norway's oldest shopping center, is located at Strandgaten 13-15, Sentrum. Visit kløverhuset.no.

Norsk Flid Husfliden

This boutique sells Norwegian handicrafts at Vågsallmenningen 3, Sentrum. Visit norskflid.no/bergen.

Xhibition Shopping Center

Xhibition offers shops, cafés, and a boutique hotel at Småstrandgaten 3, Downtown. Visit xhibition.no.

Greater Bergen

Once you've explored the bustling streets of Bergen, venture into the surrounding countryside to discover its hidden gems. Music enthusiasts flock to the homes of renowned composer Edvard Grieg and violin virtuoso Ole Bull. Another notable stop is the Fantoft Stave Church, a striking reconstruction that offers a glimpse into Viking-era architecture.

Getting Here and Around

These attractions are located farther from the city than they might seem. Consider joining a guided tour or opting for a taxi for convenient access.

Attractions

Edvard Grieg Museum

The Edvard Grieg Museum, located at Troldhaugen in Paradis, showcases the life and works of Norway's most celebrated composer. Built in 1885, this white clapboard home with green gingerbread trim was where Grieg composed many of his masterpieces. Visitors can explore a garden cottage by the lakeshore where Grieg worked and view personal mementos like his piano, paintings, and prints. Concerts are held at the adjacent Troldsalen. Entry is NKr110. The museum, situated 7 km from Bergen, is accessible at Troldhaugsveien 65. It is closed from mid-December to mid-January. For more information, call 55922992 or visit griegmuseum.no/en.

Fantoft Stave Church

The Fantoft Stave Church, originally built in 1150 in Fortun, is a reconstructed medieval wooden church famed for its dragon head details and intricate carvings. Relocated to Fantoft in 1883, the church was destroyed by fire in 1992 and later rebuilt to resemble its original structure. Visitors can reach it via light rail to Paradis, followed by a walk along Birkelundsbakken to the church. Located at Fantoftveien 38, entry costs NKr55. The church is closed from mid-September to mid-May. For details, call 55280738 or visit fantoftstavkirke.com.

Ole Bull Museum
Lysøen Island, located 25 km south of Bergen, houses the elaborate mansion of Ole Bull, a legendary violinist. Built in 1873, the house features onion domes, gingerbread gables, and cutwork trim. The property also includes 13 km of pathways ideal for picnicking, rowing, and swimming. During the summer, KODE museum in Bergen organizes guided tours. Visitors can drive or take a bus to Buena quay at Lysekloster, followed by a ferry ride. Entry to the museum and ferry costs NKr60 each. The museum is closed from mid-September to mid-May. For more information, call 56309077 or visit lysoen.no/en.

Trekking Adventures

Exploring Mount Ulriken
Mount Ulriken offers diverse trails for hikers of all skill levels. The most convenient way to the summit is via the cable car departing from Haukeland University Hospital. To reach the hospital, use the shuttle bus that operates from Torgalmenningen 1a daily from May to September. Once at the top, trails spread across the Vidden plateau, an alpine expanse connecting Mount Fløyen and Mount Ulriken. The hike between these peaks takes approximately four to six hours, providing stunning vistas along the way. However, hikers should be cautious as summer fog and rain can create hazardous conditions. For maps and advice, consult Bergen's tourist information center. For more details, contact +47 53 64 36 43 or visit www.ulriken643.no.

CHAPTER 4

SOUTHERN NORWAY

The North Sea Road offers a delightful driving experience throughout the year, featuring sunlit beaches with waters warmed by the Gulf Stream. Sandy shores transition into coastal plains, mountain peaks, and verdant forests, perfect for cycling, hiking, and mountaineering. The region's freshwater lakes, rivers, and ocean provide excellent opportunities for canoeing, kayaking, and rafting. Wildlife enthusiasts can spot beavers, deer, foxes, and a variety of birds. Southern Norway is a hub for memorable activities, from hiking Pulpit Rock to admiring the Kragerø archipelago.

Planning Your Visit

Exploring this area is straightforward, especially with a car. Towns along the North Sea Road stretch from Sandefjord in the east to Kristiansand in the south and Stavanger in the west. While smaller towns can be covered in a day, larger towns like Kristiansand and Stavanger may require additional time. Plan your itinerary based on the number of towns you wish to explore.

Best Time to Visit

The summer months, from May to August, offer the warmest and most vibrant experience, with pleasant weather ideal for outdoor activities. Despite the cold ocean waters, locals still enjoy the beaches. April and September are excellent shoulder-season alternatives, with fewer crowds and milder temperatures.

Traveling to the Region

Accessing the North Sea Road region is effortless. Multiple airports, buses, trains, and ferry options make it convenient to reach, while a scenic drive along the coastline adds to the experience.

Air Travel

Stavanger Airport is the region's main hub, with SAS Scandinavian Airlines connecting to Oslo, Bergen, Trondheim, Copenhagen, and other European cities. Norwegian Airlines offers domestic and international flights, and Flyr provides similar services. Loganair operates from Newcastle, while Wizzair connects from Gdansk and Kaunas. KLM flies from Amsterdam, and Lufthansa from Frankfurt. Kristiansand Airport, also served by SAS, Widerøe, Norwegian, and KLM, offers flights to Oslo, Bergen, and Amsterdam. Contact Norwegian at +47 21 49 00 15 or visit norwegian.com.

Ferry Services

Fjord Line operates daily car ferries between Stavanger, Bergen, Oslo, and Hirtshals, Denmark, as well as Kristiansand and Hirtshals. Color Line offers similar services between Kristiansand and Hirtshals. For details, contact Fjord Line at +47 51 46 40 99 or visit fjordline.com/nb.

Bus Transportation

Nor-Way Bussekspress provides a 10-hour route between Oslo and Stavanger and a 4.5-hour trip from Kristiansand to Stavanger. Vy offers a five-hour route between Oslo and Kristiansand, with Agder Kollektivtrafikk managing regional public buses. Contact Nor-Way Bussekspress at +47 22 31 31 50 (nor-way.no), Vy at +47 40 70 50 70 (vy.no), or Agder Kollektivtrafikk at +47 38 03 83 00 (akt.no).

Driving

From Oslo, it's 330 km to Kristiansand and 455 km to Stavanger. The E18 runs along the coast to Kristiansand, while the E39 leads inland to Stavanger. The route from Bergen to Stavanger involves two ferry crossings, operating around the clock.

Train Travel

Go-Ahead's "Sørtoget" Southern Train departs Oslo Central Station eight times daily, taking five hours to Kristiansand and eight to nine hours to Stavanger. The Kristiansand-Stavanger leg takes about three hours, with eight departures daily. For details, contact Go-Ahead at go-aheadnordic.no.

Dining in Southern Norway

Southern Norway's restaurants primarily emphasize seafood, and many offer some of the freshest fish in the region. Given that the major towns are all located on or near the coast, diners can enjoy meals with exceptional views of the water. The atmosphere at most restaurants is laid-back, meaning you don't need to worry about dressing up for dinner, though locals do tend to dress slightly more formally when they go out to eat.

Visitor Information

For more information about the region and its offerings, visit Visit Sørlandet at visitsorlandet.com, Fjord Norway at fjordnorway.com, or Visit Jæren at visitjæren.com

Rree Range Sheep in Southern Norway

Arendal

Arendal's Tyholmen, or Old Town, offers visitors a delightful blend of picturesque charm and historical richness. The narrow streets lined with wooden houses are filled with cascading flowers in shades of pink and red. A must-see landmark is the town hall, constructed in 1815. It stands as Norway's tallest timber structure and houses over 300 portraits, mainly created in the 19th century by local artists.

Getting Here and Around

Arendal is located 260 km (418 miles) south of Oslo. A drive along the E18 takes about 3 hours and 20 minutes. For public transportation, frequent bus services operated by Vy run from Oslo to Arendal.

Attractions

Bomuldsfabriken Art Gallery

The Bomuldsfabriken (Cotton Factory) is an art gallery housed in a building that originally produced cotton flannel clothing between 1898 and 1960. Today, it hosts a dynamic array of rotating art exhibitions alongside a permanent collection featuring 35 works by notable Norwegian painters. The gallery is located at Oddenveien, Arendal. Admission is NKr 100, and the gallery can be contacted at P 37-01-30-60 or through their website at bomuldsfabriken.no.

Kuben Arendal History Museum

Kuben Arendal History Museum, established in 1832, showcases an extensive collection of artifacts from coastal life, including toys, farm tools, and regional folk art. It also features exhibits on the 1767 slave ship Fredensborg. The museum is located at Parkveien 16, Arendal. Admission costs NKr 90, and the museum is closed on Mondays. For more information, visit kubenarendal.no.

Merdøgaard Skjærgårdsmuseum

Located on the island of Merdø, the Merdøgaard Skjærgårdsmuseum can be reached by a 30-minute boat ride from Arendal. The museum is housed in an early-18th-century sea captain's home and explores life in the region through various exhibits. After visiting, enjoy a swim or a walk around the island. Admission is NKr 90, and the museum operates from June to mid-August.

For more details, visit kubenarendal.no/opplev-paakuben/merdoegaard.

Restaurants

Egon Arendal
Egon offers Norwegian classics in a cozy, family-friendly setting. Outdoor seating available. Average price: NKr 250. Located at Hotel Arendal, Friergangen 1, Arendal. Contact: 37-05-21-72, egon.no/restauranter/arendal.

Hotels

Clarion Hotel Tyholmen
A maritime hotel with fjord views and central location. Breakfast included. Room rates from NKr 2100. Located at Teaterplassen 2, Arendal. Contact: 37-07-68-00, nordicchoicehotels.no.

Kristiansand

Kristiansand, known as Sommerbyen ("Summer City"), is the fifth-largest city in Norway, drawing visitors with its beautiful sunlit beaches, scenic harbor, and historical charm. The city's layout, designed by King Christian IV in 1641, is still visible in the Kvadraturen district, featuring a grid of wide streets. To the northeast lies Posebyen, a collection of wooden houses dating back several centuries, and the fish market sits at the southern edge of the grid, offering local seafood along the waterfront.

Getting Here and Around

Kristiansand is accessible from Oslo via the E18 and from Stavanger via the E39. For a unique perspective of the city, take the City Train, a 25- to 30-minute tour through the center, starting at Østre Strandgate 3. For more information, visit facebook.com/citytrainkrs.

Attractions

Agder Naturmuseum og Botanisk Hage
This museum offers an extensive look at the natural history of the Agder region, covering everything from the Ice Age to present-day ecosystems.

Visitors can explore exhibits that highlight the coastal and mountainous landscapes, a colorful mineral collection, and one of the largest collections of cacti in the country. The museum's rose garden, dating back to 1850, adds a touch of beauty to the educational displays. The museum is located at Gimle gård, Gimleveien, Kristiansand, and is open from mid-August to mid-June, with an entry fee of NKr 80. For more details, contact: 38-05-86-20 or visit naturmuseum.no.

Christiansholm Festning

Built in 1672, Christiansholm Fortress is a striking circular military structure with 16-foot-thick walls. Situated on a promontory with sweeping views of the sea, the fortress was used briefly in 1807 during the Napoleonic Wars to protect the city from a British invasion. Today, the fortress is closed to the public from mid-September to mid-May, but visitors can still admire its exterior and surroundings. The fortress is located at Østre Strandgate 52B, Kristiansand.

Dyreparken i Kristiansand

One of Norway's most beloved attractions, Dyreparken Kristiansand consists of five separate parks: a zoo, a water park, a forested park, an amusement park, and a theme park inspired by the book Kardemomme By. In the zoo, you can see native Scandinavian animals such as wolves, snow foxes, and elks, while the "My Africa" exhibition offers a safari experience with giraffes and lions. The amusement park offers thrilling rides and entertainment for all ages. The park is located 6 miles east of the city and charges NKr 649 for adult entry. It operates year-round. For more details, contact: 97-05-97-00 or visit dyreparken.no.

Gimle Gård

Gimle Gård is an elegant manor house built around 1800 in the Empire style by a wealthy merchant. The house is filled with period furnishings, portraits, chandeliers, and hand-printed wallpaper, showcasing the grandeur of the era. It is considered the most beautiful manor house in the region, offering a glimpse into the luxurious lifestyle of the time. Located at Gimleveien 23, Lillesand, the manor is open for tours from May to September, with an entry fee of NKr 110. For more information, contact: 38-12-03-50 or visit vestagdermuseet.no/gimlegard.

Kristiansand Kanonmuseum

This military museum houses a massive 15-inch cannon, originally installed by the German occupying forces during World War II. The cannon, capable of shooting projectiles as far as Denmark, is a highlight of the museum, which also showcases related military exhibits and artifacts. Visitors can explore the surrounding bunkers and enjoy the expansive grounds. However, caution is advised as there are no railings in certain areas. Located at Kroodden, Kristiansand, the museum charges NKr 110 for entry and is open from March to November, though it is closed in December and January. For further details, contact: 38-08-50-90 or visit vestagdermuseet.no/kanonmuseum.

Kristiansand Museum

This cultural museum, also known as the Vest-Agder County Museum, is the region's largest, featuring over 40 historic buildings. These structures, many of which were relocated from other parts of the region, offer a fascinating look at traditional Norwegian farm life. The museum includes two tun farm buildings, which were originally designed to house extended families. Families with children will enjoy the museum's collection of old-fashioned toys, which they can play with. The museum is located at Vigeveien 22B, Kongsgård, Kristiansand, and is open from September to May, with an entry fee of NKr 110. It is closed on Sundays in May. For more information, contact: 38-12-03-50 or visit vestagdermuseet.no/kristiansand.

Oddernes Kirke

Oddernes Church is one of Norway's oldest, dating back to 1040. The church, built on land inherited by Øyvind, godson of Saint Olav, features a beautiful Baroque pulpit from 1704. It remains an active place of worship and is free to visit. The church is located at Jegersbergvn, Kristiansand, and more details can be found at oddernes.no.

Ravnedalen

Ravnedalen is a picturesque park and nature area popular with both hikers and families. The park is especially beautiful in spring when it is filled with colorful flowers. Visitors can explore winding paths that lead up the hills, culminating in a 304-foot lookout with breathtaking views. There is a café on-site, free parking, and open-air concerts during the summer. Located in Kristiansand, the park is free to visit.

Restaurants

Sjøhuset Restaurant
A historic seafood restaurant at Strandgt. 12A, Kristiansand. Prices from NKr 390. Call 38-02-62-60 or visit wsjohuset.no.

Hotels

Clarion Hotel Ernst
Traditional hotel at Rådhusgt. 2, Kristiansand. Rooms from NKr 2000. Call 38-12-86-00 or visit nordicchoicehotels.no.

Dyreparken Hotell
Family-friendly hotel next to the zoo at Dyreparkveien 160, Kristiansand. Rooms from NKr 2500. Call 97-05-97-00 or visit dyreparken.no/overnatting/dyreparken-hotell.

TrollAktiv
Adventure center near Evje, offering activities like rafting. Open year-round. Call 37-93-11-77 or visit trollaktiv.no.

Stavanger

Stavanger's growth began in the 19th century with abundant brisling and herring, establishing it as a global sardine hub. The city's identity shifted in the 1960s with the discovery of North Sea oil, transforming Stavanger into an international and vibrant community of over 140,000 residents. Its harbor and cobblestone streets are lined with cafés, restaurants, and cultural venues, showcasing a dynamic art scene. Known as "Festivalbyen," it hosts over 20 annual festivals, including food, jazz, and literature, complemented by its renowned Michelin-starred dining.

Tours and Experiences
Explore Lysefjord, Preikestolen, and Kjeragbolten with tours by Rødne Fjord Cruise, Fjord Tours, or Norled. A seasonal hop-on/hop-off bus operates when cruise ships dock, typically June-September. For details, visit fjordtours.no or rodne.no, or contact Rødne at 51-89-52-70 and Fjord Tours at 55-55-76-60. Tours depart from Skagenkaien 35-37, Stavanger.

Visitor Information

Region Stavanger og Ryfylke provides comprehensive tourist assistance. Visit fjordnorway.com/en/destinations/the-stavanger-region or call 51-85-92-00 for more information.

Attractions

Arkeologisk Museum i Stavanger (Museum of Archaeology)

This museum is tailored to spark children's interest in prehistory through interactive exhibits, engaging models, and educational films. Visitors can enjoy activities like treasure hunts, fossil exploration, and ancestor research via computer games. Traditional toys and games also add a nostalgic touch. Located at Peder Klows Gate 30A in Stavanger, it charges NKr 100 for admission and is open Monday through Saturday from September to April. For more information, call 51-83-26-00 or visit am.uis.no.

Breidablikk

Breidablikk is a well-preserved 19th-century manor showcasing Swiss-style architecture with Norwegian Romantic influences. Built in 1882 by merchant Lars Berentsen, it features an authentic interior that offers a glimpse into the past. Situated at Eiganesveien 40A, admission costs NKr 100. It is closed from mid-August to mid-June. For details, call 51-84-27-00 or visit breidablikkmuseum.no.

Gamle Stavanger (Old Stavanger)

This historic area, the largest preserved wooden house settlement in northern Europe, consists of 150 charming houses built in the late 1700s and early 1800s. Stroll along its cobblestone streets and admire the white houses and craft shops with terra-cotta roofs. The area is located near Strandgate in Stavanger.

Iddis Norsk Grafisk Museum og Norsk Hermetikkmuseum (Norwegian Printing and Canning Museum)

Set in a former canning factory in Gamle Stavanger, this museum highlights the city's canning industry from the 1890s to the 1960s. Visitors can occasionally join production demonstrations and sample freshly smoked brisling. The museum now includes exhibits on Norway's printing history. Located at Øvre Strandgate 88, admission is NKr 100, with free entry for children under 18. It is closed from mid-August to mid-June. Contact 45-87-

38-46 or visit iddismuseum.no for more information.

Jernaldergården

This reconstructed Iron Age farm replicates ancient living conditions, complete with structures built on original foundations. Visitors can explore Bronze Age relics and enjoy Viking-era mead, breakfast, or lunch by roaring fireplaces. Situated at Madlamarkveien 152, entry costs NKr 100. The site operates Monday to Saturday from September to May. Call 51-83-26-00 or visit uis.no/nb/arkeologisk-museum for details.

Lysefjorden

Lysefjorden, a stunning fjord near Stavanger, is best appreciated by boat. Highlights include Pulpit Rock's towering cliffs and the iconic Kjerag Boulder. Tours are available from Stavanger to capture the beauty of these natural wonders.

Norsk Oljemuseum (Norwegian Petroleum Museum)

Shaped like an offshore oil platform, this museum offers an in-depth look at Norway's oil history, from its discovery in 1969 to its impact on the economy. The museum features interactive exhibits, films, and a reconstructed oil platform complete with sounds and smells of drilling. The on-site café, operated by Bølgen og Moi, serves meals and light snacks. Located at Kjeringholmen in Stavanger, entry is NKr 150. For details, call 51-93-93-00 or visit norskolje.museum.no.

Preikestolen (Pulpit Rock)

This iconic cliff rises 2,000 feet above Lysefjord, offering breathtaking views. Visitors can either take a boat tour from Stavanger to see it from below or hike two hours to the top along a marked trail starting at Preikestolhytta, which has a spacious parking area.

Solastranden

This 2.3-kilometer sandy beach near Sola is ideal for windsurfing and beach volleyball. Other notable beaches in the Jærstrendene region include Bore, Hellestø, Refsnes, Orre, and Ogna, with Ølberg, Vigdel, Vaulen, Godalen, and Viste Stranden offering family-friendly options. Public transport is limited to most beaches, but trains from Stavanger can reach Ogna and Brusand, about 60 kilometers away. Solastranden is located at Axel Lunds Veg 23 in Stavanger.

Stavanger Kunstmuseum (Stavanger Art Museum)
Located by Lake Mosvatnet, around 3 kilometers from Stavanger's city center, this museum features a notable collection of 19th- and 20th-century Norwegian art, including works by Lars Hertervig. The Halvdan Hafsten Collection showcases pieces from between the world wars. Situated at Henrik Ibsens Gate 55, admission is NKr 100. The museum is closed Mondays from mid-August to mid-June. Contact 93-21-37-15 or visit stavangerkunstmuseum.no for details.

Stavanger Maritime Museum
This museum occupies two historic shipping merchants' houses, dating back to 1770-1840. Exhibits explore 200 years of maritime trade, shipbuilding, and sea traffic. Visitors can see a reconstructed general store, a merchant's apartment, and a sailmaker's loft. Outside, the sloop Anna af Sand and the Colin Archer yacht Wyvern are moored at the pier. Located at Strandkaien 22, admission is NKr 100. It is closed Mondays from mid-September to mid-May. For more information, call 51-84-27-00 or visit stavangermaritimemuseum.no.

Sverd i Fjell (Swords in Rock)
This iconic monument at Møllebukta in Hafrsfjord commemorates Norway's unification under King Harald Fairhair after the 872 Battle of Hafrsfjord. Designed by Fritz Røed and unveiled in 1983, the three bronze swords symbolize the different Norwegian districts involved.

Utstein Kloster (Utstein Abbey)
Norway's best-preserved medieval monastery, dating back to the late 1200s, is located on Mosterøy, about a 30-minute drive from Stavanger. Accessible by car or bus, the abbey is near Åmøy Island, where visitors can explore medieval ruins, Stone Age carvings, and the Fjøløy Lighthouse. Admission costs NKr 100, and the abbey is closed from November to February and Mondays to Saturdays in September, October, and April. For details, contact 51-84-27-00 or visit utsteinkloster.no.

Restaurants

Harry Pepper
Tex-Mex meets Norwegian cuisine in a lively setting with cacti and souvenirs. Skagenkaien 33, Stavanger. Mains NKr300, lunch Thurs-Sat. harry-

pepper.no, 51-89-39-59.

HN.B. Sørensens
A historic wharf turned waterfront restaurant offering Norwegian fare. Skagen 26, Stavanger. Mains NKr275, lunch Sat. nbsorensen.no, 51-84-38-26.

XO Steakhouse
Traditional Norwegian dishes, steaks, and burgers in a casual pub setting. Skagen 10, Stavanger. Mains NKr400, closed Sun-Mon. xosteakhouse.no, 91-00-03-07.

Hotels

Clarion Skagen Brygge
Classic harbor-view hotel with complimentary meals and cozy rooms. Skagenkaien 28-30, Stavanger. Rooms NKr2000. nordicchoicehotels.no, 85-00-00.

Clarion Hotel Stavanger
Modern downtown hotel with fitness facilities and 24-hour service. Arne Rettedals gt. 14, Stavanger. Rooms NKr1600. nordicchoicehotels.no, 51-50-25-00.

Radisson Blu Atlantic
Central hotel with spacious rooms and a sauna overlooking Breiavatnet. Olav Vs gt. 3, Stavanger. Rooms NKr1400. radissonhotels.com, 51-76-10-00.

Victoria Hotel
Historic hotel blending Victorian charm and modern comforts. Skansegt. 1, Stavanger. Rooms NKr1300. victoria-hotel.no, 51-86-70-00.

Nightlife

Bøker og Børst
Quirky café and pub with artwork and a cozy garden in Øvre Holmegate. Holmegate 32, Stavanger. bokerogborst.business.site.

Folken
Concert venue hosting music, art, and cultural events. Løkkeveien 24,

Stavanger. folken.no, 51-56-44-44.

Shopping

Sølvsmeden
Top spot for exquisite jewelry and watches. Sølvberggt. 5, Stavanger. solvsmeden.no, 51-89-42-24.

Syvende Himmel
Retro boutique offering colorful, alternative fashion. Øvre Holmegt. 21, Stavanger. Call 51-01-29-61.

Outdoor Adventures

Guided Hiking in Stavanger
Stavanger Turistforening offers detailed maps and guidebooks to explore the scenic trails around the Setesdalsveiene Hills and the Ryfylke Archipelago, known for their rugged beauty and abundant islands. Their office provides assistance for trip planning and offers access to 45 member cabins for overnight stays. Located at Olav Vs gt. 18, Stavanger, they also allow membership registration on-site. Visit stf.no or call 51-84-02-00 for details.

Southern Actor Museum Ship

Risør

One of the best-preserved wooden towns in Europe, Risør is a picturesque coastal destination steeped in a rich history of boatbuilding. Its charming streets and vibrant maritime culture make it a delightful place to visit for history enthusiasts and nature lovers alike.

Getting Here and Around

Risør is accessible by car, situated just under three hours from Oslo. For train travel, the nearest station is Gjerstad, located 35 km (22 miles) away and served by Go-Ahead's Sørtoget line connecting Oslo and Kristiansand. Visitors arriving by train can take a taxi or bus from Gjerstad Station to Risør.

Attractions

Risør Akvarium
This saltwater aquarium, the only one in southern Norway, features over 500 marine species visible through large glass panels. Popular activities include feeding the fish and viewing Norway's largest lobster. Located at Strandgate 14, Risør, entry costs NKr120. Open weekdays mid-August to mid-June. Visit risorakvarium.no or call 41-64-87-59 for more details.

Risør Fiskemottak
Situated near fishing trawlers and warehouses, this market is where daily fresh catches are brought in. Visitors can explore unique fish varieties, shop at the fish store, and dine at the outdoor restaurant. Find it at Solsiden 3, Risør. For more information, visit fiskemottaket.no or call 37-15-23-50.

Lillesand

Lillesand is a picturesque coastal town known for its vibrant harbor, often filled with locals enjoying boating excursions. The town's charming streets are lined with the region's signature white wooden houses, adding to its idyllic appeal.

Getting Here and Around

Lillesand is accessible by car via the E18 highway, which passes through the municipality. During summer, visitors can travel between Lillesand and Kristiansand by boat, with several stops along the route. The town is a 3½-hour drive from Oslo and just 30 minutes from Kristiansand by car.

Attractions

Høvåg Church
This historic church, originally built around AD 1000, has undergone multiple expansions, with its current stone structure finalized in 1966. Located at Bliksundveien 64, Høvåg, Lillesand, it remains an architectural treasure. For more information, visit hovag.org or call 489-55-788.

Lillesand Town and Maritime Museum
Housed in a stately Empire-style building from 1827, this museum showcases the region's maritime heritage, including exhibits on sailmaking and the town's first fire pump. Located at Nygårdsgata 1, Lillesand, admission is NKr50. The museum is closed Mondays and from mid-August to mid-June. Visit lillesandmuseet.com or call 46-81-75-10 for details.

Restaurants

Harry Pepper
Located at Skagenkaien 33, Stavanger, Harry Pepper serves Tex-Mex dishes with a Norwegian twist. Average main NKr300. Open Thursday-Saturday for lunch. Call 51-89-39-59 or visit harry-pepper.no.

HN.B. Sørensens Dampskibsexpedition
This waterfront restaurant at Skagen 26, Stavanger offers a mix of Norwegian history and creative cocktails. Average main NKr275. Lunch on Saturdays only. Call 51-84-38-26 or visit nbsorensen.no.

XO Steakhouse
At Skagen 10, Stavanger, XO Steakhouse offers seafood, Angus burgers, and grilled steaks. Average main NKr400. Closed Sundays and Mondays, lunch on Saturdays. Call 91-00-03-07 or visit xosteakhouse.no.

Clarion Collection Hotel Skagen Brygge
A central hotel at Skagenkaien 28-30, Stavanger, with views of the harbor and free breakfast. Rooms from NKr2000. Call 85-00-00 or visit

nordicchoicehotels.no.

Clarion Hotel Stavanger
Located at Arne Rettedals gt. 14, Stavanger, this hotel offers comfortable rooms and fitness facilities. Rooms from NKr1600. Call 51-50-25-00 or visit nordicchoicehotels.no.

Radisson Blu Atlantic Hotel
With views of Breiavatnet Pond, this downtown hotel offers rooms from NKr1400. Call 51-76-10-00 or visit radissonhotels.com.

Victoria Hotel
Located at Skansegt. 1, Stavanger, Victoria Hotel offers stylish accommodation with free breakfast. Rooms from NKr1300. Call 51-86-70-00 or visit victoria-hotel.no.

Bøker og Børst
This cozy pub at Øvre Holmegate 32, Stavanger serves drinks in a vibrant setting. Visit bokerogborst.business.site.

Folken
A live music venue at Løkkeveien 24, Stavanger, featuring local and international acts. Call 51-56-44-44 or visit folken.no.

Sølvsmeden på Sølvberget
Located at Sølvberggt. 5, Stavanger, this is the city's top jewelry store. Visit solvsmeden.no.

Hotels

Syvende Himmel
This shop at Øvre Holmegt. 21, Stavanger specializes in retro and alternative clothing. Call 51-01-29-61.

Hos Oss på Fiskebrygga
At Strandgata 18, Lillesand, this seafood restaurant offers live concerts in summer. Average main NKr250. Call 32-27-02-03 or visit facebook.com/hosossfiskebryggalillesand.

Hotel Norge
A harbor-side hotel at Strandgaten 3, Lillesand with great views. Rooms from NKr1600. Call 37-01-44 25 or visit [hotelnorge.no](http://hot

Sandefjord

Sandefjord, a renowned coastal city in Norway, has attracted visitors, particularly those from Oslo, since the 1800s due to its appeal as a spa destination. The city was once dominated by trading and whaling, with remnants of its maritime past still visible today. Although Sandefjord can be quite busy during the summer months, the vibrant restaurant scene, specializing in local seafood, and boat excursions along the stunning coastline offer ample rewards.

Getting Here and Around

Sandefjord is easily accessible from Oslo via bus, and several daily trains run along the Vestfoldbanen line. The E18 highway passes through the municipality, providing a quick 90-minute drive from Oslo to Sandefjord, making it an ideal location for a short getaway.

Attractions

Bryggekapellet Church
The Bryggekapellet Church, Europe's only floating church, is an iconic sight in Sandefjord. Visitors can light a candle or simply enjoy the soothing sounds of the waves beneath. It is open for six weeks each summer. You can find it at Brygga 1, Sandefjord, Vestfold og Telemark. For more information, visit sandefjord.kirken.no or call +47 33 47 62 52. The church is closed from September to May.

Hvalfangstmonumentet (Whaling Monument)
This striking monument, designed by Knut Steen, stands proudly in Sandefjord and has become a symbol of the city's whaling heritage. Surrounded by graceful plumes of water, the monument rotates continuously, offering visitors a captivating experience. It is located at Indre Havn, Sandefjord, Vestfold og Telemark.

Hvalfangstmuseet (Whaling Museum)

The Hvalfangstmuseet is the only museum of its kind in Europe, dedicated to the history of whaling and the study of whales. The museum's centerpiece, a life-size model of a blue whale, is especially captivating for children. The building, established in 1917, houses a wealth of historical exhibits. The museum is open from October to April, excluding Easter. You can find it at Museumsgt. 39, Sandefjord, Vestfold og Telemark. Visit vestfoldmuseene.no/hvalfangstmuseet or call +47 33 41 79 33 for further details. The museum is closed on Mondays.

Kragerø

Kragerø is a beloved destination for many Norwegians, particularly those who dream of owning a hytte (cabin) here. Known for its picturesque scenery, boats are the primary mode of transportation in the town. The central street functions as a channel where boats dock, allowing visitors to explore the area and enjoy dining at the many charming restaurants. The combination of natural beauty and maritime life makes Kragerø an idyllic spot for both locals and tourists.

Getting Here and Around

To reach Kragerø from Oslo or Kristiansand, drive along E18 until you reach Gjerdemyra, then follow Route 38 into the heart of the town. Once in Kragerø, you can take a boat to explore the larger islands of the archipelago. For those coming by bus, the nearest stop is Neslandsvatn Station in Drangedal, a short distance from Kragerø.

Attractions

Berg - Kragerø Museum

The Berg Kragerø Museum is housed in a charming Louis XVI-style manor built in 1803 by the Homann family. This historic home offers a fascinating glimpse into family life and the popular cabin life tradition in Norway. The museum also features an exhibit on artist Edvard Munch, who spent time in Kragerø. The museum is open for concerts and guided tours during the off-season and can be visited by groups and individuals. It is located at Lovisenbergveien 45, Kragerø, Vestfold og Telemark. For details, visit telemarkmuseum.no/berg-kragero-museum or call +47 35 54 45 00.

The museum is closed from September to mid-June.

Jomfruland National Park
Jomfruland National Park, easily accessible by ferry from Kragerø, offers an excellent way to explore the archipelago and its wildlife. Established in 2016, the park spans 117 square kilometers (45 square miles) and includes the islands of Jomfruland and Stråholmen, with the majority of the park area being ocean. Visitors should be cautious around the sand dunes, as small creatures inhabit the area. The park is located in Kragerø, Vestfold og Telemark. For more information, visit jomfrulandnasjonalpark.no.

Kittelsen House
Kittelsen House, the childhood home of renowned Norwegian artist Theodor Kittelsen, is now a museum. Known for illustrating children's stories and fairy tales, Kittelsen's work holds a special place in Norwegian culture. The museum is located at Th. Kittelsens Vei 5, Kragerø, Vestfold og Telemark. For more information, visit telemarkmuseum.no/kittelsenhuset or call +47 35 54 45 00. The museum is closed on Mondays and from September to May.

Bjoreio River in southern Norway

CHAPTER 5

CENTRAL NORWAY

Central Norway is renowned for its extraordinary natural beauty. While the fjords are iconic, the inland landscapes are equally mesmerizing, earning this region the title "Heart of Norway." As you move northward from Oslo, the terrain becomes more dramatic with rolling hills that give way to steeper mountains. The charming valleys of Valdres and Gudbrandsdalen are dotted with traditional farming villages and striking wooden stave churches, set against a backdrop of lush greenery. This area also features an artistic touch with sculptures integrated into nature as part of the Kunstlandskap Gudbrandsdalen initiative.

If you're keen on exploring Norway's wilderness, you'll find yourself surrounded by three major national parks: Rondane, Jotunheimen, and Dovrefjell-Sunndalsfjella. These parks are home to emerald lakes, fast-flowing rivers, vast plateaus, and towering peaks that seem to touch the sky. The region enjoys a drier climate, with warm, sunny summers and cold winters, making it ideal for outdoor enthusiasts. Hiking, biking, rock climbing, glacier walking, canoeing, white-water rafting, and skiing are popular activities in the area, drawing locals and tourists alike.

Best Time to Visit Central Norway

Central Norway's temperate inland climate makes it an attractive destination throughout the year. Summer temperatures are perfect for mountain hikes, while early fall offers vibrant forest colors. The high season is from mid-June to August, though mountain lodges often open in May and close after September. Spring and fall, the shoulder seasons, offer pleasant weather and fewer tourists. Winter enthusiasts can enjoy skiing from November to April.

How to Get to Central Norway and Get Around

Air Travel
Oslo Airport is the main international gateway for reaching Central Norway.

Boat Travel
Mjøscharter offers scenic boat rides across Lake Mjøsa, providing a faster alternative to road travel. For instance, the boat ride from Hamar to Helgøya takes only 10 minutes, compared to a 50-minute drive. For details, visit destinasjonsservice.no or call +47 48 39 54 49.

Bus Travel
Nor-Way Bussekspress connects Central Norway with Lillehammer and the Valdres region. Innlandstrafikk provides local bus services throughout the region. In winter, ski buses run to various alpine and cross-country resorts, while summer buses take visitors to mountain resorts along the Rondane National Tourist Route. For more information, visit innlandstrafikk.no or call +47 91 50 20 40, or visit nor-way.no or call +47 23 31 31 50.

Car Travel
Driving is one of the best ways to explore Central Norway, as you'll find many hidden villages along winding roads. The E6 runs from Oslo to Lillehammer and other towns in Gudbrandsdalen Valley. For a scenic detour, take Route 27 from Ringebu to Venabygdsfjellet, part of the Rondane National Tourist Route. The main road through Valdres is E16, leading to Fagernes, with Route 51 continuing to Beitostølen. In winter, a four-wheel drive vehicle is recommended, especially for icy conditions.

Train Travel
Regional and local trains offer convenient service between Oslo and Lillehammer, with frequent departures. Trains heading north toward Trondheim provide a scenic journey through Gudbrandsdalen Valley. Trains are also available from Oslo Airport. For more information, visit vy.no or call +47 61 05 19 10.

Dining in Central Norway

Central Norway's cuisine is heavily influenced by the region's abundance of fish and game. Local specialties include lamb, reindeer, Arctic char, perch, and trout, often paired with berry or mushroom-based sauces. The area's fresh ingredients and traditional cooking methods provide a delicious taste of Norwegian culinary culture.

Where to Stay in Central Norway

Accommodation in Central Norway offers a range of options, from modern hotels to historic guesthouses. Many villages and mountain areas feature charming lodges with stunning views. For a unique experience, consider staying in the igloo-shaped tents at Arctic Dome Sjusjøen, the 700-year-old Sygard Grytting farm in Gudbrandsdalen, or the Elgtårnet moose observation tower. In the national parks and surrounding areas, the Norwegian Trekking Association operates both staffed and unstaffed lodges. For more details, visit dnt.no.

Visitor Information

Located in Otta, Nasjonalparkriket offers information on several national parks, including Rondane, Dovre, Dovre-Sunndalsfjella, Reinheimen, Breheimen, and Jotunheimen. For more information, visit nasjonalparkriket.no or call +47 61 24 14 44.

Røros

Founded in 1646 after the discovery of copper ore, Røros became a significant mining hub, and over the centuries, its rich heritage has shaped its unique character. This vibrant town is renowned for its well-preserved wooden architecture, narrow streets, and charming ambiance. In 1980, Røros was designated a UNESCO World Heritage Site, a testament to its historical importance. The town comes alive during summer, but December holds a magical allure, with sparkling lights and a lively market transforming it into a fairy-tale setting. Visitors can explore cozy cafés, unique shops, and a wide range of traditional arts and crafts.

Getting to Røros and Local Transportation

Røros is easily accessible by several means of transport. The town is served by Røros Airport, which has daily flights from Oslo. If traveling by car, Røros is a two-hour drive from Trondheim via Route RV30, and a five-hour drive from Oslo through E6 and RV3. For train enthusiasts, there are regular tra services from Oslo, except on Saturdays. Most of the local attractions are within walking distance, though taxis and buses are available for those seeking more convenience. For taxi services, contact Røros Taxi at Johan Falkbergets vei 2, Røros, Innlandet, phone number 72-41-12-58.

Visitor Information

For additional information and assistance during your stay, the Røros Tourism Office is located at Peder Hiortgata 2, Røros, Innlandet. They can be reached at 72-41-00-00 or via their website at www.roros.no.

Attractions

Røros Kirke (Røros Church)
Built during the prosperous years of the Røros Copper Company, Røros Church is one of Norway's largest churches, with a seating capacity of 1,600. Completed in 1784, its white-and-green tower stands out above the town's rooftops. Following an extensive restoration in 2010, the church remains a major historical and architectural landmark. Located at Kjerkgata 39, Røros, Innlandet, visitors can explore this grand structure for an admission fee of NOK 50. The church is closed weekdays from September 12 to May 1. For more information, visit www.roroskirke.no or call 72-41-98-11.

Rørosmuseet Olavsgruva (Olav's Mine)
Olav's Mine, part of the Røros Copper Works, offers a fascinating glimpse into the region's mining history. The mine, which operated from 1937 to 1972, was the last of its kind in the area. Visitors can take a guided tour 50 meters underground to explore the mine's tunnels, lit by dim lights and crossed by wooden walkways. The mine's temperature hovers just above freezing, so warm clothing and sturdy shoes are recommended. The site is not wheelchair accessible due to stairs. Located at Gruveveien 612, about 13 km east of Røros in Glåmos, Innlandet, tours are priced at NOK 180. The mine is closed from Sunday to Wednesday, and on Fridays and Sundays during mid-September to May. For more details, visit www.rorosmuseet.no or call 72-40-61-70.

Rørosmuseet Smelthytta (Røros Museum Smelthytta)
Smelthytta, built on the site of a smelter that burned down in 1975, offers insights into the history of the Røros Copper Works. The museum features

exhibits with models of mines and mining equipment. Guided tours are available, along with audio guides in English. Located at Malmplassen, Røros, Innlandet, the entrance fee is NOK 130. For more information, visit www.rorosmuseet.no or call 72-40-61-70.

Activities

Røros, located 630 meters above sea level, offers a variety of outdoor activities throughout the year, including hiking, biking, and cross-country skiing.

Biking
Røros Guide provides guided biking and hiking tours for all skill levels, or you can rent a bike and explore on your own. Located at Tollef Bredals vei 11, Røros, Innlandet, this outfitter is ideal for both beginners and experienced adventurers. For more information, visit www.rorosguide.no or call 977-61-521.

Dogsledding
Røros Husky Tours offers an exciting dogsledding experience, where you can either mush your own team of dogs or enjoy the ride as a passenger wrapped in reindeer skins. The tours take you through the stunning mountains surrounding Røros. Located at Ormhaugen Gård, Røros, Innlandet, more information is available at www.roroshusky.no or by calling 915-15-228.

Skiing
Røros boasts over 300 miles of groomed ski trails, along with vast mountain plateaus for those wishing to create their own routes. Skiing season typically runs from November to May, providing ample opportunity for both recreational and seasoned skiers.

Røros Sport AS
For all your skiing and snowboarding needs, Røros Sport AS offers rentals of top-quality skis and snowboards. Located at Bergmannsgata 13, Røros, Innlandet, the store is closed on Sundays. For more information, visit their Facebook page at Røros Sport or call 72-41-12-18.

Hamar

Located on the northeast shore of Lake Mjøsa, Hamar holds deep historical significance, once serving as the seat of a bishopric during the Middle Ages. The city's landmark, four Romanesque arches, remains a symbol of its rich heritage. These arches are part of the wall of a former cathedral. The 13th-century monastery ruins also stand as a testament to the city's religious history, now housing a glassed-in exhibition showcasing regional artifacts, including items from the Iron Age. Hamar, the largest city in Norway's interior, boasts a diverse range of attractions and serves as an important hub for those exploring central Norway.

Getting to Hamar and Local Transportation

Hamar is easily accessible for travelers flying into Oslo, with train services connecting the two cities in about an hour. Trains depart from Oslo Airport every hour, with the journey from Oslo Central Station taking approximately 90 minutes. Additionally, there are several daily buses from Oslo to Hamar. If traveling by car, take the E6 for a direct route.

Skibladner Paddle Steamer

Skibladner, the world's oldest paddle steamer still in operation, was launched in 1856 and is affectionately known as the "White Swan of the Mjøsa." This historic vessel offers daily summer departures from Hamar, connecting nearby towns along the lake. During the week, the steamer travels as far as Lillehammer three days a week and stops at Eidsvoll on other days. The beautifully restored saloons for gentlemen and ladies add to the nostalgic charm. Skibladner departs from Brygga 31, Innlandet, and can be reached at 61-14-40-80 or through www.skibladner.no.

Visitor Information

For information about Hamar and the surrounding region, the Hamar Tourism Office is located at Strandgata 45, Innlandet. They can be contacted at 40-03-60-36 or by visiting their website at visitmjosa.no.

Attractions

Domkirkeodden (Cathedral Point)
Located in Hamar, Cathedral Point is home to the remains of a medieval cathedral, including four Romanesque arches that form the focal point of the site. The modern glass structure built over these ruins offers a striking contrast, making it one of Europe's most unique museum buildings. Visitors can explore 50 grass-roofed houses from the region, depicting life in historic Hamar. Additionally, the site features an organic garden with 350 varieties of herbs. The museum is located at Strandveien 100, Hamar, and can be contacted at 62-54-27-00. Admission is 140 Kr, and it is closed from mid-September to mid-May. For more details, visit www.domkirkeodden.no.

Eidsvollsbygningen (Eidsvoll House)
Eidsvoll House is a key symbol of Norwegian history, being the site where the country's Constitution was signed in 1814. Situated a 50-minute drive south of Hamar, the neoclassical house and its surrounding park offer a glimpse into Norway's past. The museum includes the house itself, several additional buildings, and a charming café with outdoor seating. The address is Carsten Ankers veg 19, Eidsvoll Verk, and they can be reached at 63-92-22-10. Admission costs 140 Kr, and the site is closed on Mondays from September to April. Visit www.eidsvoll1814.no for more information.

Hamar Olympiahall (Hamar Olympic Hall)
Hamar Olympic Hall, shaped like an inverted Viking ship, was the venue for speed-skating and figure-skating events during the 1994 Lillehammer Winter Olympics. The best way to experience the venue is by attending a sporting event, where visitors can witness the stadium's full grandeur. It is located at Åkersvikvegen 1, Innlandet, and can be contacted at 62-51-75-00. More details can be found at vikingskipet.com.

Norsk Jernbanemuseum (Norwegian Railway Museum)
This railway museum, one of Europe's oldest, opened in 1896 and showcases

Norway's rail history. The museum features train memorabilia and offers an outdoor display of locomotives and carriages on narrow-gauge tracks. From mid-May to mid-August, visitors can enjoy a ride on Tertittoget, the last steam locomotive built by Norway's state railway. The museum is located at Strandveien 161, Innlandet, and can be reached at 40-44-88-80. Admission is 140 Kr, and it is closed on Mondays from January to May and again from September to December. Visit www.jernbanemuseet.no for more details.

Beach

Koigen Beach

Koigen Beach is a modern beach area just a short walk from Hamar's city center, offering a sandy beach, an artificial island, basketball courts, volleyball courts, skateboarding facilities, and a well-equipped playground. The beach walk is scenic year-round, with amenities including food, drinks, and toilets. It is ideal for sunset views, surfing, swimming, and walking. Koigen is located approximately 500 meters from the city center. For more information, visit visitmjosa.no.

Restaurants

Heim Gastropub Hamar

Heim Gastropub is known for its delicious creamed mussel soup and other local specialties. The average main dish price is 230 Kr, and it is located at Torggata 41, Hamar. Contact them at 62-80-94-20 or visit heim.no/hamar.

Kai & Mattis Café

Kai & Mattis Café stands out with its bright red interior and is renowned for its delicious homemade lunches and extraordinary soft serve. The average main dish costs 200 Kr, and it is located at Torggata 53, Hamar. For inquiries, call 62-53-01-45 or visit www.facebook.com/kaiogmattis.

Activities

Boating with Infoteket

Infoteket, located about a 50-minute drive from Hamar, offers boat and kayak rentals, as well as guided tours and courses during the summer months. It is one of the best places to rent boats on Lake Mjøsa. Infoteket is situated at Tingnesveien 796, Innlandet, and can be reached at 47-16-59-13. More details are available on www.infoteket.no. Note that the service is closed during winter.

Hedmarksvidda Husky

Hedmarksvidda Husky offers year-round dogsledding and other outdoor activities, providing an authentic way to experience Norway's wilderness. Located at Ellevsætervegen 637, Innlandet, the company can be contacted at 92-86-04-10. For more information, visit www.hedmarksviddahusky.no.

Traditional graveyard with church in central Norway

Dombås

Located in the far northern part of Gudbrandsdalen Valley, Dombås serves as an excellent base for exploring Dovrefjell-Sunndalsfjella National Park. This small village offers easy access to the scenic train ride to Åndalsnes, providing a perfect starting point for nature lovers and adventurers.

Getting Here and Around

Dombås is accessible by car via the junction of E6 and E136, located 4½ hours north of Oslo and 3 hours south of Trondheim. The Dovre Railway connects Oslo and Trondheim with several daily stops in Dombås, making it easy to reach. The train ride from Oslo takes approximately four hours.

Visitor Information

To preserve the wild reindeer herds in Dovrefjell, access to Snøheim, a key starting point for hikes in the park, is only possible via the Snøheim Shuttle Bus. This shuttle runs five times daily from late June to early October. The Dombås Tourist Information Center can be reached at nasjonalparkriket.no, while the Snøheim Shuttle Bus departs from Hjerkinnhusveien 33, Hjerkinn, and can be contacted at 47-86-22-86. For more information, visit snoheim.dnt.no/snoheimvegen.

Attractions

Dombås Kyrkje (Dombås Church)
Located in the heart of Dombås, this charming church was constructed in 1939 and designed by architect Magnus Poulsson. The church features a cruciform design and is distinguished by its striking wooden altarpiece, which showcases ten intricate paintings portraying the life of Jesus. Situated at Kyrkjevegen 6, Dombås, the church can be reached at 61-24-14-44. It remains closed from early August to late June. For more details, visit visitdovrefjell.no/dombs-kirke.

Dovrefjell-Sunndalsfjella Nasjonalpark
Dovrefjell-Sunndalsfjella National Park is renowned for its dramatic landscapes, ranging from the alpine scenery of the northwest to the drier, rounded mountains in the east. The park's highlight is Mt. Snøhetta, standing

at 2,286 meters (7,500 feet), previously thought to be Norway's highest peak. It is now ranked 24th, after Jotunheimen in Rondane National Park. The park is home to wild reindeer, musk oxen, and Arctic foxes, and both Kongsvold/Reinheim and Hjerkinn are excellent starting points for hiking. For further information, visit nasjonalparkriket.no.

Snøhetta Viewpoint

The Snøhetta Viewpoint, part of the Norwegian Wild Reindeer Centre Pavilion, offers stunning vistas of Mt. Snøhetta and Dovrefjell-Sunndalsfjella National Park. Designed by the Snøhetta architectural agency, this pavilion provides a warm, dry spot to rest and take in the surrounding views. With some luck, visitors may even spot musk oxen and wild reindeer. The viewpoint is accessible via a hiking trail from the Snøhetta parking lot or the Hjerkinn train station. Open from June to mid-October, the viewpoint offers free entry. It is closed from October to May. For more details, visit villrein.no.

Hotels

Dombås Hotel

Situated at the base of the Dovrefjell Mountains, Dombås Hotel is centrally located near village shops and restaurants. Rooms start at NKr1595, with free breakfast. Address: Domaasgrendi 1, Dombås, phone 61-24-10-01. Visit dombas-hotell.no.

Furuhaugli Turisthytter

Nestled in Dovrefjell-Sunndalsfjella National Park, Furuhaugli Turisthytter offers a peaceful setting with rooms starting at NKr1250, featuring kitchenettes. Address: Furuhauglie 80, Dombås, phone 61-24-00-00. Visit furuhaugli.no.

Hjerkinn Mountain Lodge

This historic mountain lodge, run by the same family for generations, offers rooms from NKr1670, with free breakfast. Address: Kvitdalsvegen 12, Hjerkinn, phone 61-21-51-00. Visit hjerkinn.no.

Dovre Handverkstugu

Located in an old schoolhouse in Dombås, Dovre Handverkstugu offers traditional crafts like knitted sweaters. Closed on Sundays. Address: Bondegardsvegen 1, Dombås, phone 48-17-38-43. Visit facebook.com/dovrehandverkstugu.

Activities

Biking in Dovre
The Tour de Dovre bike trail offers cyclists the chance to explore both Dovrefjell-Sunndalsfjella and Rondane National Parks. Starting in Dombås, the 32 km (20 miles) gravel road leads to Hjerkinn.

Dovrefjell Adventures
Located at Nordre Stasjonsveg 26, Dombås, Dovrefjell Adventures rents bikes, canoes, and offers guided excursions such as moose safaris. For more information, call 45-45-66-33 or visit dovrefjelladventures.no.

Hiking in Dovrefjell
Dovrefjell-Sunndalsfjella National Park spans 4,367 square kilometers (1,686 square miles) and is perfect for hiking. The diverse terrain features rounded hills to sharp peaks, with Snøhetta, the tallest peak, being a popular hiking destination.

Furuhaugli Musk Ox Safari
For an unforgettable wildlife experience, join a guided safari to observe the musk oxen in Dovrefjell. Guided tours increase the chances of seeing these magnificent creatures and reindeer. The safari costs NKr695 and departs from Furuhaugli 80, Dovrefjell-Sunndalsfjella National Park. Visit furuhaugli.no for more details.

Otta

Otta is a small city located where the Otta River meets the Gudbrandsdalslågen River in northern Gudbrandsdalen Valley. Positioned between Rondane and Jotunheimen National Parks, it offers a great base for exploring the region, with the Sjoa River nearby for white-water rafting.

Getting Here and Around

Otta is a three-hour drive from Oslo Airport and lies along the E6 highway. The Dovre Railway connects Oslo to Otta in 3½ hours, while the bus ride takes around five hours. Rondane National Park's main access points, Mysuseter and

Høvringen, are 30 minutes away by car. Many local hotels offer shuttle services to Otta.

Contacts

For more information, visit the Otta Tourism Office at Ola Dahls gt. 1, Otta. For inquiries, call 61-24-14-44 or check the nasjonalparkriket.no website.

Attractions

Kvitskriuprestein

The Kvitskriuprestein, or White Priests, are natural stone pillars in the Uladalen Valley near Otta. These towering geological formations are unique to northern Europe, with the tallest reaching nearly 20 feet and more than 200 years old. The site is located off the E6, about 4 km (2 miles) north of Otta in Innlandet.

Rondane National Park

Rondane National Park, Norway's first national park, features 10 peaks over 2,000 meters (6,561 feet) in the north, along with expansive moors and rolling hills in the southeast. Popular trails include those to Rondeslottet and Storronden, while the Bridal Veil waterfall offers a stunning 4 km (2½ miles) hike from Mysusæter Entrance. The park is accessible via Fv 444, Rondane National Park, Innlandet. For more information, visit nasjonalparkriket.no or call 61-24-14-44.

Restaurants

Pillarguri Café

Located in downtown Otta, this century-old café offers dishes featuring local ingredients like trout and moose. Average main: NKr150. Storgata 7, Otta, Innlandet. Call 61-23-01-04. Visit pillarguricafe.no.

Spiseriet Rondane

Spiseriet Rondane serves local delicacies like reindeer fillet and mountain trout. Average main: NKr300. Rondane Høyfjellshotell, Rondanevegen 1264, Mysusæter, Innlandet. Call 61-20-90-90. Visit rondane.no.

Activities

Hiking in Rondane National Park
Rondane National Park offers a variety of hiking experiences, with ten summits above 2,000 meters. The highest peak, Rondeslottet at 2,178 meters, provides a 360-degree view if the weather is clear. The popular route from Rondvassbu takes around five hours and passes Vinjeronden. Storronden, at 2,138 meters, offers panoramic views of the surrounding peaks and plains. For families, the Veslesmeden peak, at 2,013 meters, is one of the easiest high-altitude hikes, boasting views of Rondeslottet and Jotunheimen on clear days.

Rondaneguiden
Rondaneguiden provides guided hiking, skiing, and snowshoeing tours through Rondane National Park, catering to various skill levels. Electric bicycles are available for rent during summer months. Rondaneguiden is located at Ola Dahls gt. 1, Otta, Innlandet. Contact them at 94-09-40-04. Visit rondaneguiden.no.

White-Water Rafting on the Sjoa River
The Sjoa River, just 20 minutes from Otta, is known for its thrilling white-water rafting experiences through narrow canyons and turbulent rapids. It offers guided trips suitable for all skill levels, with an option for more relaxed rafting on the Otta River.

Sjoa Rafting
Sjoa Rafting offers family-friendly expeditions on the Sjoa River, ranging from a few hours to a full day. Other activities include canyoning, riverboarding, and SUP. The season runs from May to October, with options to stay in lavvus or cottages. Sjoa Rafting is located at Rte. 257, off E6, Nedre Heidal, Innlandet. Call 90-07-10-00. Visit sjoarafting.no.

Ringebu

Ringebu, often referred to as Norway's smallest city, offers visitors a charming experience with its historic stave church, art gallery, and sculptures nestled in nature. The town features local shops selling regional art and delicacies. For those looking to explore the area, Dølabike rents out electric bicycles, providing a great way to navigate the picturesque hills of Gudbrandsdalen and the nearby Gudbrandsdalslågen River. Just outside Ringebu lies Venabygdsfjellet in Rondane National Park, as well as the mountain villages of Gålå, Skåbu, and Espedalen. Ringebu is also home to the Kvitfjell ski arena, which hosted the 1994 Winter Olympics' downhill events.

Getting Here and Around

Ringebu is located about 2½ hours from Oslo Airport. You can travel by train, bus, or car along the E6 highway.

Attractions

Ringebu Prestegard (Ringebu Rectory)
Located just a three-minute walk north of the Ringebu Stave Church, the 1743 Ringebu Rectory offers a breathtaking view of the Gudbrandsdalslågen River and surrounding mountains. Now a museum and gallery, the rectory houses six buildings, with the main building serving as a gallery for the works of renowned Norwegian artist Jakob Weidemann. Visitors can also explore a spacious garden filled with perennials and over 150 rosebushes. It's located at Ringebu Prestegard, Ringebu, Innlandet. For more details, call +47 61 28 79 50 or visit www.ringebustavkirke.no/prestegarden. Admission is NOK 100, and the site is closed from mid-September to May.

Ringebu Stavkyrkje (Ringebu Stave Church)
The stunning Ringebu Stave Church, situated 2 km south of the town, is one of Norway's largest remaining stave churches. Built in the 1220s and rebuilt in 1630 after the Lutheran Reformation, it features a striking red tower completed in 1631. The church was first painted in 1717 and was once entirely white. In 1921, renovations restored the original colors. Inside, visitors can admire a statue of St. Laurentius from around 1250. The church is located at Ringebu Stavkyrkje, Ringebu, Innlandet. For more information, call +47 61 28 08 74 or visit www.stavechurch.no. Admission is NOK 80, and it is closed from late August to mid-May.

Hotels

Elgtårnet i Espedalen
This 40-foot tower offers scenic views, but requires a 30-minute walk. No electricity or running water. Located at Espedalsvegen 2346, rooms from NOK 3000. Call +47 908 37 773 or visit www.elgtarn.no.

Skåbu Mountain Hotel
A family-run hotel with luxurious rooms and a restaurant. Located at Skåbuvegen 23-207, rooms from NOK 2100. Call +47 61 29 55 00 or visit www.skabufjellhotell.no.

Venabu Mountain Hotel
Set at the edge of Rondane National Park, offering local cuisine and heated floors. Located at Rondevegen 860, rooms from NOK 1700. Call +47 61 29 32 00 or visit www.venabu.no.

Performing Arts

The Peer Gynt Festival
Held in August in Gålå, featuring "Peer Gynt" and cultural events. Located at Valsetervegen 10, tickets from NOK 745. Call +47 959 00 770 or visit www.peergynt.no.

Shopping

Annis Pølsemakeri
Rustic shop with sausages, jams, cheeses, and beers. Located at Tomtegata 10, Ringebu, closed Sundays. Call +47 61 28 03 54 or visit www.polsemakeri.no.

Activities

Dalseter Mountain Lodge Canoe Rental
Located near Lake Breidsjøen in Espedalen, Dalseter Mountain Lodge offers canoe, SUP, and small rowboat rentals. This is a great way to explore the tranquil waters in the beautiful surroundings of the area. The lodge is situated at Espedalsvegen 2346, Espedalen, Innlandet. For reservations or further details, call +47 61 29 99 10 or visit www.dalseter.no.

Venabu Mountain Hotel Guided Walks
Venabu Mountain Hotel provides guided walks tailored to your level of experience. You can choose a leisurely stroll around the plateau or embark on a more challenging summit hike. They also offer assistance with cross-country skiing, dogsledding, and sleigh rides. The hotel is located at Rondevegen 860, Venabygd, Innlandet. For more information, call +47 61 29 32 00 or visit

www.venabu.no.

Kvitfjell Alpine Resort

From November to May, Kvitfjell Alpine Resort offers some of the best skiing in the region, with over 20 miles of slopes, two family areas, two terrain parks, and a dedicated free-riding area called Powder Wood. The resort is located at Kvitfjellvegen 47, Fåvang, Innlandet, around 45 minutes from Lillehammer. For more details, call +47 61 24 90 00 or visit www.kvitfjell.no.

Oslo Central Station Trains

Beitostølen

Located at the edge of Jotunheimen National Park, Beitostølen is a prime destination for winter enthusiasts, offering reliable snow from November to May. In the warmer months, this quaint mountain village transforms into an excellent base for hiking adventures in the surrounding peaks.

Traveling to Beitostølen
Reaching Beitostølen is convenient from Oslo. The Valdresekspressen bus service connects Oslo Central Station to the village in under four hours, passing through the scenic Begnadalen Valley. By car, the journey takes approximately three hours via E16 and Route 51. Within Jotunheimen National Park, vast areas can be accessed from Beitostølen in the Valdres Valley or Otta in the Gudbrandsdalen Valley. Local buses operate in summer, linking visitors to popular hiking trails.

Guided Tours and Excursions
For a unique experience, the historic Bitihorn boat offers trips on Lake Bygdin, showcasing over 10 peaks in Jotunheimen that soar above 2,000 meters. Wildlife enthusiasts may even spot reindeer during the journey. Another option is the Gjendebåten ferry, which traverses Gjende Lake, connecting Gjendesheim in the west to Gjendebu in the east.

Contact Information
Beitostølen Tourism Office is located at Bygdinvegen 3780, Beitostølen, Innlandet (phone: 61-35-94-20, website: valdres.no). For the Bitihorn boat, visit Jernbanevegen 7, Fagernes (phone: 61-36-16-00, website: jvb.no). Gjendebåten ferry services are available at Øygardsvegen 187, Vågå, Innlandet (phone: 913-06-744, website: gjende.no).

Attractions

Beitostølen Lyskapellet (Beitostølen Light Chapel)
This captivating chapel, adorned with unique painted glass creations by the late Norwegian artist Ferdinand Finne, is a remarkable architectural gem. Located at Sentervegen 2, Beitostølen, Innlandet, the chapel is a tranquil space that blends art and spirituality. For more information, visit valdres.no.

Besseggen Ridge
Renowned as Norway's most frequented day hike, Besseggen Ridge attracts approximately 60,000 hikers annually. Situated in Jotunheimen National Park, the trail runs between the alpine lakes of Gjende and Bessvatnet, offering stunning vistas. The ideal period for the hike is from mid-June to mid-October when the Gjendebåten boat operates. Hikers can park at Reinsvangen and take the shuttle bus to Gjendeosen, where the boat departs. For more details, contact 61-24-14-44 or visit nasjonalparkriket.no.

Jotunheimen Nasjonalpark (Jotunheimen National Park)
Established as a haven for hiking and mountaineering since the 19th century, Jotunheimen National Park is home to northern Europe's highest concentration of peaks over 2,000 meters, including Galdhøpiggen and Glittertind. Aptly named "Home of the Giants," the park also boasts several lakes, with Gjende being the largest. Its extensive trail network caters to all skill levels. For information, call 61-24-14-44 or visit nasjonalparkriket.no.

Valdresflye National Tourist Route
This scenic drive across the Valdresflye mountain plateau offers breathtaking views, with numerous stops to photograph the landscape or embark on mountain hikes. During summer, nearby farms provide traditional food for sale. Note that the route is closed from December to March. For more details, visit nasjonaleturistveger.no.

Hotels

Hindsæter Mountain Hotel
Located in Sjodalen Valley, this hotel offers 26 rooms with saunas and a whirlpool. Rooms start at NKr1650 with breakfast. Sjodalsveien 1549, Tessanden, Innlandet. Call 61-23-89-16 or visit hindseter.no.

Jotunheimen Mountain Lodge
Near Jotunheimen Park, this lodge has 18 rooms with scenic views and a restaurant. Rooms from NKr1600 include breakfast. Sognefjellsvegen, Bøverdalen, Innlandet. Call 61-21-29-18 or visit jotunheimen-fjellstue.com.

Nordre Ekre Farm Hotel
This 7-room hotel in Heidal offers tranquility and mountain views. Rooms start at NKr1695 with breakfast. Heidalsvegen 1265, Innlandet. Call 481-20-866

or visit nordre-ekre.no.

Radisson Blu Mountain Resort Beitostølen
Close to ski trails, this hotel features 124 rooms and a spa with a pool. Rooms begin at NKr2050 with breakfast. Bygdinvegen 3812, Beitostølen, Innlandet. Call 61-35-30-00 or visit radissonblu.com.

Lillehammer

Situated by Lake Mjøsa, Lillehammer serves as the entry to Gudbrandsdalen Valley and showcases preserved 19th-century wooden houses along Storgata. Known for hosting the 1994 Winter Olympics, it features active venues, ski resorts with cross-country trails, and summer hiking and biking opportunities.

Getting Here and Around
Lillehammer is under two hours from Oslo Airport by car, train, or bus via E6. Most nearby resorts are accessible within 90 minutes.

Tours
Lillehammer Guide Union offers free 60- to 90-minute city walks and two-hour guided tours. Visit facebook.com/LillehammerGuideforening for more information.

Visitor Information
Lillehammer and Gudbrandsdalen Tourism Office at Jernbanetorget 2 provides regional details. Call 61-28-98-00 or visit lillehammer.com or gvegen.no for further guidance.

Attractions

Aulestad
Visit the home of Bjørnstjerne Bjørnson, renowned writer and politician, located 20 minutes from Lillehammer. The residence, preserved as it was in his time, showcases Karoline Bjørnson's art collection. Open from June to September, admission costs 140 NOK. Located at Aulestadvegen 6-14, Innlandet. For more details, call 61-28-89-00.

Bjerkebæk

Explore the historic home of Nobel laureate Sigrid Undset, featuring two Gudbrandsdalen log houses and 1930s interiors. Open from June to September, entry is 140 NOK. Visit Bjerkebæk, Sigrid Undsets veg 16E, Innlandet. Contact 61-28-89-00 or check bjerkebek.no for updates.

Hunderfossen Familiepark

This amusement park, 13 km north of Lillehammer, features a giant troll, a fairy-tale castle, rides, and exhibits. Admission is 411 NOK, with seasonal operation from June to August. Located at Fossekrovegen 22, Innlandet. Call 61-27-55-30 or visit hunderfossen.no.

Lillehammer Kunstmuseum

The Lillehammer Museum of Art, with works by Munch and Tidemand, includes a sculpture garden and modern architecture by Snøhetta. Open Tuesday to Sunday from September to May, tickets cost 140 NOK. Find it at Stortorget 2, Innlandet. Call 61-05-44-60 or visit lillehammerartmuseum.com.

Maihaugen

Maihaugen, Europe's largest open-air museum, showcases Norway's history through historic buildings, crafts, and seasonal markets. Admission starts at 140 NOK, with reduced hours from September to May. Located at Maihaugvegen 1, Lillehammer. For details, call 61-28-89-00 or visit maihaugen.no.

Norges Olympiske Museum

Discover Olympic history from ancient Greece to modern times at this museum, featuring multimedia exhibits and interactive displays. Open Tuesday to Sunday, with entry at 140 NOK from September to April. Located at Maihaugvegen 1, Lillehammer. Contact 61-28-89-00 or visit ol.museum.no.

Olympiaparken

Experience Olympic thrills with ski jumps, bobsledding, and simulators at this iconic park. Open year-round with seasonal activities; details vary. Visit Birkebeinervegen 122, Lillehammer, or call 61-05-42-00. For more, check olympiaparken.no.

Restaurants

Bryggerikjelleren
Located in a 1855 brewery cellar, Bryggerikjelleren offers premium steaks in an intimate setting. Average main: 400 NOK. Address: Elvegata 19, Lillehammer. Phone: 61-27-06-60. Closed Sundays and Mondays. No lunch.

Heim Gastropub
Heim Gastropub serves homemade burgers, fish-and-chips, and Norwegian specialties. Average main: 235 NOK. Address: Storgata 84, Lillehammer. Phone: 61-10-00-82. No lunch weekdays.

Hvelvet
Hvelvet offers upscale dining in the former Norwegian Bank with a warm atmosphere. Average main: 345 NOK. Address: Stortorget 1, Lillehammer. Phone: 907-29-100. Closed Sundays. No lunch.

Hotels

Arctic Dome Sjusjøen
For a luxury glamping experience, stay in an igloo-shaped tent at Sjusjøen. Rooms from: 2800 NOK. Address: Sjusjøvegen, Sjusjøen. Phone: 94-84-62-70. Includes canoes; no meals.

Clarion Collection Hammer Hotel
Clarion offers cozy rooms, a gym, and an evening meal included. Rooms from: 1990 NOK. Address: Storgata 108, Lillehammer. Phone: 61-26-73-73. Free breakfast.

Mølla Hotell
Mølla Hotell is a charming hotel with a homey feel. Rooms from: 1980 NOK. Address: Elvegt. 12, Lillehammer. Phone: 61-05-70-80. Free breakfast.

Scandic Lillehammer Hotel
Scandic features a spa, wellness area, and family-friendly amenities. Rooms from: 2000 NOK. Address: Turisthotellvegen 6, Lillehammer. Phone: 61-28-60-00. Free breakfast.

Activities

Hafjell Bike Park
Hafjell Bike Park, located just 20 minutes from Lillehammer, offers downhill biking with 18 trails for all levels of riders. You can access the trails via the gondola or chair lift, and the park provides bike rentals and protective gear on-site. Prices start from 330 NOK. Address: Hundervegen 122, Øyer, Innlandet. Phone: 40-40-15-00. Open June to October, closed November through May. For more details, visit www.hafjell.no.

Nordseter Fjellpark
Nordseter Fjellpark provides mountain bike, canoe, and kayak rentals during summer months, along with cross-country skiing lessons in winter. Address: Nordsetervegen 1361, Lillehammer, Innlandet. Phone: 994-37-000. Visit www.nordseter.no for further information.

Sjusjøen Husky Tours
Experience dogsledding with Sjusjøen Husky Tours, located 30 minutes from Lillehammer. In summer, the tours transition to wheels. Address: Sjusjøvegen, Mesnali, Innlandet. Phone: 94-84-62-70. More details are available on www.sjusjoenhuskytours.no.

Gålå Alpin
Gålå Alpin, 89 km north of Lillehammer, is an excellent destination for families who enjoy both alpine and cross-country skiing. The resort features eight lifts and 14 slopes in addition to cross-country trails in stunning surroundings. Address: Børkdalsvegen 1, Gålå, Innlandet. Phone: 48-10-02-40. Closed from mid-November to mid-April. Visit www.gala-alpin.no for more details.

Hafjell Alpine Resort
Located just 15 minutes from Lillehammer, Hafjell Alpine Resort offers family-friendly slopes alongside more challenging runs for thrill-seekers. The resort features 18 lifts and 33 slopes, including a gondola. Address: Hundervegen 122, Øyer, Innlandet. Phone: 40-40-15-00. Closed mid-April through mid-November. For more information, go to www.hafjell.no.

Fagernes

Fagernes, nestled on the shimmering Strondefjorden, derives its name from two Norwegian words: "fager," meaning beautiful, and "nes," meaning headland. The town is a perfect representation of its name, situated in one of Norway's most picturesque regions. It serves as an excellent base for exploring Jotunheimen National Park and offers a variety of local attractions, including the open-air Valdres Folkemuseum.

Navigating Fagernes

To get to Fagernes, you can drive via E16 from Oslo and Bergen, or take Route 250 or Route 33 from Lillehammer. The Valdresekspressen express bus operates up to eight times daily between Oslo and Fagernes, with additional daily services from Bergen and Lillehammer.

Contacts

For taxi services, contact Fagernes Taxisentral at Jernbanevegen 13, Fagernes, Innlandet. Phone: 61-36-18-00. Visit www.fagernestaxi.no for more details. The Fagernes Tourism Office, located at Jernbanevegen 7, Fagernes, Innlandet, can be reached at 61-35-94-10 or via www.valdres.no.

Attractions

Hedalen Stave Church

Dating back to approximately 1163, Hedalen Stave Church is a medieval gem nestled in the town of Hedalen. It is renowned for its intricately designed wooden reliquary, shaped like a miniature church, a rare find in Norway. Inside, the Hedal Madonna sculpture from the 1200s stands out as one of the finest pieces of medieval ecclesiastical art. Visit Hedalsvegen, Hedalen, Innlandet, with admission priced at NOK 60. It is closed Tuesdays and from mid-August to late June. More details can be found at stavechurch.com.

Valdres Folkemuseum

The Valdres Folkemuseum, located on a scenic peninsula extending into Strondefjord, is a remarkable open-air museum spanning 30 acres. The museum features over 100 historic structures, including a 1300s wooden warehouse with medieval ornaments. Inside, the modern building showcases exhibits on bunader (Norwegian traditional costumes), folk instruments, and vintage toys. Guided tours, available in July and August, should be booked in advance. Located at Tyinvegen 27, Fagernes, Innlandet, the entry fee is NOK 120. It is closed on Mondays from October to June. More information can be found at valdresmusea.no.

Activities

Intersport Fagernes
Intersport Fagernes offers a wide range of sports gear for sale, along with bicycle rentals. Due to its popularity, it's advised to make reservations in advance for bike rentals. Located at Gullsmedvegen 2, Fagernes, Innlandet, the shop is closed on Sundays. For more details, call 61-36-29-40.

Jotunheimen Travel
Jotunheimen Travel offers guided and self-guided hiking tours in Jotunheimen, where you can explore some of the region's most popular hiking routes. The company is based at Fagernes Skysstasjon, Jernbanevegen 7, Fagernes, Innlandet. You can reach them at 91-11-11-33, or visit jotunheimentravel.com for more information.

Myhre Gård
Myhre Gård offers horseback riding excursions for all skill levels, ranging from two-hour trips to multi-day treks. It's located at Nordheimveien 12, Skammestein, Innlandet. For bookings, call 915-20-232 or visit myhregard.com for more details.

Dalsnibba Fjord Mounatins, Norway

QUICK NOTE

"I hope this chapter proved informative. Your feedback on the book thus far is highly valued and will be used to enhance future editions. Please take a moment to share your thoughts by dropping a review on Amazon. Thank you, and enjoy the rest of the book."

CHAPTER 6

OSLOFJORD

During the summer months, many residents of Oslo head to the tranquil coastal towns on the east coast of Oslofjord for a peaceful retreat. These picturesque towns are easily accessible by car, bus, or train, and ferries often provide direct access from the city's downtown docks. The harbor areas are bustling with interesting restaurants and shops, perfect for those looking to enjoy the charm of these communities. To the west of Oslo, towns that are seldom explored by tourists are home to some of Norway's oldest and wealthiest communities, built on a history of whaling and lumbering. Museums in this area offer a deep dive into this proud heritage.

Best Time to Visit

Oslofjord experiences a typical Scandinavian climate, with summer lasting from May to September. This is when most locals flock to their cabins by the fjord. For a quieter experience, visiting in the shoulder seasons, either early spring or late fall, offers fewer crowds but may result in some closures. It's essential to plan ahead, and consider renting an electric car to truly experience the region's beauty, with numerous charging points scattered across the area.

Exploring the Region

While several towns along Oslofjord are perfect for a day trip from Oslo, the farther you travel, the more time you'll want to spend there. A night in each village is usually enough to take in the atmosphere and surrounding landscapes. Ferries allow you to cross between islands and fjords with ease, making it possible to complete a full loop of the Oslofjord region without backtracking. Norway's transport system ensures convenience and flexibility.

Getting Around

For visitors, there's no need to drive as regular trains and buses depart daily from Oslo Station to coastal towns like Drøbak and Fredrikstad. However, renting an electric car gives you the flexibility to explore more distant areas and stop by local farms, galleries, and workshops. The region is well-equipped with charging stations, making it easy to travel sustainably.

Dining by the Water

Dining in Oslofjord typically revolves around seafood, and many of the best eateries are situated along the waterfront. Since many restaurants only operate during the summer months, it's wise to call ahead if traveling in the off-season. Be prepared for premium pricing, as these locations serve some of the finest fresh seafood alongside hearty comfort food.

Accommodation Options

Accommodation in the Oslofjord region is less dominated by hotel chains, with a focus on more personalized experiences. In addition to the budget-friendly Scandic hotels offering impressive breakfast spreads, you'll find family-run bed-and-breakfasts providing a cozy, intimate atmosphere with welcoming staff and homey touches like candles at breakfast. For those seeking luxury, spa hotels with forest-set bathhouses, outdoor pools, and health-focused restaurants provide a perfect getaway. Note that many accommodations close during the winter, so it's important to book in advance.

Visitor Information

For more details about the area, you can visit the official websites: Visit Greater Oslo and Visit Østfold.

Bærum

Bærum, a trendy suburb located just 20 minutes from Oslo, is predominantly residential but offers a hidden gem along the Lomma River—Bærums Verk. In the 1960s, the owners of the former Bærums Verk iron foundry transformed the area into a historical site, preserving its industrial past. Visitors can explore this charming district, with its quaint wooden cottages on Verksgata, once home to factory workers. These buildings are uniquely designed with rear-facing doors to prevent the spread of fire, a legacy from the days when industrial accidents were a constant threat. Alongside the workshops and exhibitions, the village continues to captivate with its rich history and scenic views.

Attractions

Henie Onstad Art Center

Often referred to as the "MoMA of Oslofjord," Henie Onstad Art Center boasts Norway's largest collection of international modern art. The museum's collection began when Sonja Henie, a renowned skater, and her husband, shipping magnate Niels Onstad, acquired early-20th-century masterpieces, including works by Munch, Picasso, Bonnard, and Matisse. The highlight of the collection is a permanent installation of a pumpkin infinity room by Japanese artist Yayoi Kusama. The museum's ultramodern, minimalist architecture, designed by Norwegian architects Jon Eikvar and Sven Erik Engebretsen, blends seamlessly into the picturesque surroundings of Oslofjord. Additionally, visitors can enjoy the museum's sculpture park, a children's play area, and an excellent on-site restaurant. Located at Sonia Henies Vei 31, Bærum, the museum charges an entry fee of NOK 120. It is closed on Mondays and can be reached at +47 67 80 48 80. For more details, visit Henie Onstad Art Center.

Museum of Bærums Verk

This museum showcases an impressive collection of cast-iron ovens manufactured at the Bærums Verk iron foundry from the 18th century until its closure in the mid-20th century. The museum offers fascinating tours of its exhibits, available in English, where visitors can learn about the industrial heritage of the region. Located at Verksgata 15, Bærums Verk, entry is free. For more information, visit Museum of Bærums Verk.

Drøbak

Drøbak, a picturesque town just a short drive from Oslo, offers a glimpse of southern Norway's coastal charm with its colorful wooden houses and winding cobblestone streets. Although only 30 minutes from the capital, this town provides a serene escape for locals, who often visit for beach days and to indulge in freshly caught shrimp at the waterfront restaurants. Drøbak boasts several captivating attractions, including Oscarborg Festning, an island fortress with a fascinating history tied to the sinking of the German battleship

Blücher in the fjord. Families will also appreciate a visit to Drøbak Akvarium, where kids can marvel at the local marine life.

Getting Here and Around

Drøbak is easily accessible by car, bus, or train. A 20-minute drive from Oslo, you can take the E18 or E6 south, then switch to the E134 for the final stretch to the waterfront. For a more scenic approach, you can take a one-hour ferry ride from Oslo's Aker Brygge to Drøbak, available from May to September. If driving, the journey takes just over half an hour, making Drøbak an ideal day trip for anyone staying in Oslo. Its well-preserved waterfront is best experienced by boat, offering an unforgettable view of this coastal gem.

Visitor Information

For more details about visiting Drøbak, visit Visit Drøbak.

Attractions

Drøbak Akvarium (Drøbak Aquarium)

This charming aquarium, located at Havnegata 4 in Drøbak, features 14 tanks filled with marine life from the fjords. Kids will enjoy getting close to creatures like Morgan the deep-sea eel and Hugo the catfish. The giant basins allow visitors to touch colorful starfish, often collected by the manager, Klaus Bareksten. Admission costs NOK 70. For more information, visit Drøbak Akvarium or call +47 91 10 84 20.

Drøbak Båthavna (Drøbak Harbor)

Drøbak Harbor is home to three bronze mermaids sitting on rocks near the water. Created by Norwegian artist Reidar Finsrud, these sculptures are a playful and local favorite. The harbor is located not far from Drøbak Akvarium, making it easy to visit both attractions in one trip. The harbor is situated at Havnegata in Drøbak.

Drøbak Gjestehavn (Drøbak Marina)

Drøbak Marina offers stunning views of the fjord and is one of the first sights visitors encounter upon arriving in the town. The marina is home to Sjøstjernen, one of the region's most popular restaurants. Drøbak's marina can be found at Badehusgata.

Drøbak Kirke (Drøbak Church)
Drøbak Church, built in 1764, is nestled within the lush Badeparken. This wooden church features boat sculptures, nautical mobiles, and a royal balcony overlooking the pews. Its Gothic altar and a blue-and-white painted ceiling add to the charm of the small but impressive space. The church is located at Kirkegata 18, Drøbak. For inquiries, call +47 64 90 61 70.

Friluftsmuseet (Open-Air Museum)
The Open-Air Museum, an extension of the Follo Museum, is located at Belsjøveien 17 in Drøbak. This museum showcases old houses from the Oslofjord area, displaying the region's history and contemporary arts. It's a family-friendly destination, although it is closed on Mondays. For more details, visit Follo Museum or call +47 66 93 66 36.

Oscarsborg Festning (Oscarsborg Fortress)
Accessible by ferry from Drøbak or Oslo, Oscarsborg Fortress is a must-see historic site. Once regarded as Europe's strongest fortress, it was instrumental in sinking the German battleship Blücher in 1940. The fortress, located on an island in the fjord, offers tours of its military history, museum, and stunning views. Visitors can enjoy lunch at the fjordside cafeteria or dine at the Oscarsborg Hotel's restaurant. For more information, visit Oscarsborg Fortress Museum or call +47 81 55 19 00.

Tusenfryd Amusement Park
Located at Fryds Vei 25 in Vinterbro, Tusenfryd Amusement Park is Norway's oldest amusement park and boasts over 30 thrilling rides, including the ThunderCoaster, Europe's steepest wooden roller-coaster. The park operates daily during the summer and on weekends in the spring and fall. A shuttle bus from Oslo Bussterminalen Galleriet departs regularly for the park. Admission is NOK 329. For further details, visit Tusenfryd or call +47 64 97 64 97.

Restaurants

Cafe Sjøstjernen
Located at Badehusgata 27, Drøbak, Cafe Sjøstjernen offers a Norwegian menu with fjord views. The modern concrete-and-glass design enhances its appeal. Average main dishes cost NOK 180. Contact +47 90 75 61 15 for details.

Det Gamle Bageri Ost & Vinstue
Housed in an 18th-century red wooden building, this eatery at Havnebakken 1, Drøbak, serves Norwegian dishes like salmon with sweet-mustard sauce. Average mains cost NOK 220. Visit detgamlebageri.no or call +47 64 93 21 05.

Kumlegården
Located at Niels Carlsens Gate 11, Drøbak, Kumlegården serves a mix of seafood, forest, and farm-inspired Norwegian cuisine. Average mains are NOK 240. Contact +47 64 93 89 90 for more details.

Skipperstuen
Skipperstuen at Havnebakken 11, Drøbak, specializes in fresh seafood dishes like salmon carpaccio. Average mains are NOK 220. Visit skipperstuen.no or call +47 64 93 07 03. Closed Mondays and Tuesdays.

Telegrafen
Telegrafen at Storgata 10, Drøbak, offers a restored historic setting with fjord views and tasty desserts. Average mains cost NOK 250. Visit telegrafendrobak.no or call +47 915 25 359.

Hotels

Oscarsborg Hotel
Situated in Oscarsborg Festning, this hotel features historic charm and fjord views. Rooms start at NOK 1300, including breakfast. Visit festningshotellene.no or call +47 64 90 40 00.

Reenskaug Hotel
Reenskaug Hotel at Storgata 32, Drøbak, combines historic charm with a central location. Rooms start at NOK 1039, with breakfast included. Visit reenskaug.no or call +47 64 98 92 00.

Shopping

Galleri Finsrud
Located at Badeveien 12, Drøbak, Galleri Finsrud showcases diverse art styles and features Finsrud City, a detailed motion model. The gallery is closed Sundays. Visit galleri-finsrud.no or call +47 64 93 23 99.

Tregaarden's Julehus (Christmas House)
At Havnebakken 6, Drøbak, this Christmas shop offers ornaments, toys, and cards designed by Eva Johansen. Open year-round, it embodies festive charm. Visit julehus.no or call +47 64 93 41 78.

Fredrikstad

Norway's oldest fortified city, Fredrikstad, sits peacefully where the Glomma River meets the sea. Its 17th-century bastions and moat provide a glimpse into its rich history, while the charming Gamlebyen, or Old Town, captivates visitors with half-timbered houses, moats, and drawbridges.

Getting Here and Around

Fredrikstad is accessible from Drøbak, Son, or Oslo, with driving via the E6 taking about an hour. Alternatively, a train from Oslo Central Station offers a slightly longer journey. Once in Fredrikstad, park your car and explore on foot. Be sure to enjoy the free ferry that connects the old and new parts of the city.

Visitor Information
For details, contact Visit Fredrikstad and Hvaler at +47 69 30 46 00 or visit visitfredrikstadhvaler.com/en.

Attractions

Fredrikstad Domkirke (Fredrikstad Cathedral)
This grand neo-Gothic cathedral, built in 1860, stands at Riddervoldsgate 5 in the town center. Its stunning stained-glass windows, designed by Emanuel Vigeland, also adorn Oslo Cathedral. For information, call +47 69 95 98 00.

Fredrikstad Museum
Located at Tøihusgaten 41, this museum chronicles the city's evolution from

the 16th century onward. It's particularly engaging for children, offering activities like toy-making. Admission costs NOK 80, and hours vary, so call +47 69 11 56 50 or visit ostfoldmuseene.no/fredrikstad.

Restaurants

Big Fish Cafe
At Torvet 6, Fredrikstad, this family-run eatery serves fresh seafood platters with a lively terrace. Mains average NOK 220. Contact +47 69 37 88 00 or visit bigfishcafe.no; closed Mon.-Thurs.

Første Reis
Located at Under Kollen 2, Fredrikstad, this spot offers modern takes on Norwegian classics and an extensive wine list. Mains cost around NOK 208. Call +47 919 17 733 or visit forste-reis.no.

Majorens Kro
At Voldportgaten 73, this seafood and game restaurant offers a popular game buffet. Mains average NOK 250. Contact +47 69 32 15 55 or visit majoren.no.

Hotels

Gamlebyen Hotell
Located at Voldportgaten 72, this boutique hotel features themed rooms starting at NOK 1258. Call +47 400 53 909 or visit gamlebyenhotell.no.

Shopping

Glashütte
At Torsnesvn. 1, this studio offers handmade glassware and custom pieces. Contact +47 48 09 52 39.

Halden

Halden is a charming town with a rich history, highlighted by its role in Norwegian-Swedish border conflicts. The town's most famous event was the death of King Karl XII at Fredriksten Fortress in 1718. Its historical attractions and scenic surroundings make it a worthwhile destination.

Getting Here and Around

Halden is accessible by train or bus from Oslo, Fredrikstad, and nearby coastal towns. The E6 highway offers a direct drive from Fredrikstad in about 40 minutes.

Visitor Information

For information, contact Visit Halden at +47 69 19 09 80 or visit visitoestfold.com/en/halden.

Attractions

Fredriksten Fortress

Fredriksten Fortress, located at Generalveien 27, Halden, was built in the late 1600s as a defense against Swedish invaders. It features exhibits on historical conflicts, a pharmacy showcasing folk medicine, a bakery once serving 5,000 men, and the Fredriksten Kro pub with outdoor seating. For more information, call +47 69 11 56 50 or visit visithalden.com.

Rød Herregård (Red Manor House)

Rød Herregård, situated at Herregårdsveien 10, Halden, is an 18th-century manor surrounded by Baroque and English gardens. It houses period furniture, hunting trophies, and a weapons collection. Guided tours are available three times daily from May to September, with a café and gallery open during summer. Contact +47 69 11 56 50 or visit visitoestfold.com/no/halden/artikler/Rod-Herregard; closed October through April.

CHAPTER 7

WESTERN FJORD

Norway's 21,347 km coastline, shaped by intricate fjords, offers breathtaking views and majestic landscapes. Fjords like Nærøyfjord and Geirangerfjord, both UNESCO World Heritage Sites, showcase towering cliffs, snowcapped peaks, and cascading waterfalls. The rugged northern fjords, such as Sognefjord, Nordfjord, and Geirangerfjord, present stunning natural beauty, with features like Europe's largest glacier and unique rock formations.

Planning Your Visit

Given the rural nature of the region, planning ahead is essential. Research routes, road conditions, and transportation options to maximize your experience. Renting a car offers the most flexibility, though public transportation is available with careful planning.

Best Time to Visit

The fjords are captivating year-round. Summer (June to August) is the busiest season, with most services fully operational. Spring and autumn (April, May, September, October) provide quieter visits, while winter (November to March) offers serene landscapes but limited services and transportation.

Getting Here and Around

Exploring fjords by boat is iconic but limited to coastal areas. To fully experience the countryside, a car is highly recommended. Public transport is an option but requires thorough preparation to accommodate schedules and routes.

Attractions

Hardangerfjord Area
Home to Trolltunga and two national parks, this region is a paradise for hikers. Its historic significance is reflected in an 1848 painting of a couple rowing across the fjord, a testament to its timeless allure. Visit hardangerfjord.com for details.

Sognefjord Area
The continent's longest fjord spans 200 km, featuring Jotunheimen and Jostedalsbreen national parks. Popular in summer, it attracts climbers and glacier hikers to its stunning landscapes. Visit sognefjord.no for more information.

Nordfjord Area
Nestled between Sognefjord and Geirangerfjord, this region boasts picturesque villages like Olden and Loen. It's ideal for photographers, nature enthusiasts, and hikers. Learn more at nordfjord.no.

Geirangerfjord Area
Recognized by UNESCO, this fjord is famed for waterfalls like Seven Sisters and Bridal Veil. Restored mountain farms, such as Skageflå, add cultural depth to the natural splendor.

Nordvestlandet
Stretching from Kristiansund to Selje, this coastal area features jagged mountains and islands. Known for its fishing heritage, it also offers some of Norway's most accessible scenic spots. Visit visitnorthwest.no for guidance.

FjordSafari Tours
Explore Aurlandsfjord and Nærøyfjord aboard a RIB boat for a close encounter with nature. Guided by skilled drivers, these tours offer an intimate experience with stops for wildlife sightings. Contact +47 99 09 08 60 or visit fjordsafari.com.

Visitor Information
For regional insights, explore hardangerfjord.com, nordfjord.no, visitnorthwest.no, or sognefjord.no.

Åndalsnes

In The Bat, Jo Nesbø wrote that God spent extra time perfecting Åndalsnes, leaving it a masterpiece of natural beauty. Known as "the Mountain Peak Capital," this area is surrounded by dramatic, snow-covered peaks that captivate visitors. Åndalsnes serves as the final stop on the railway and a gateway to Norway's fjord region. Notable landmarks include the Trollstigen (Troll Ladder), a winding mountain road, and the Trollveggen (Troll Wall), Europe's tallest vertical rock face and a hub for rock climbing in Scandinavia.

Getting Here and Around

Molde Airport, located 90 minutes from Åndalsnes, offers daily flights from Oslo, Bergen, and Trondheim. Daily buses also connect Åndalsnes with Bergen and Trondheim. For train travel, the Raumabanen line runs from Oslo to Åndalsnes in approximately 5.5 hours. If traveling by car, follow the E136 through the picturesque Romsdalen Valley.

Attractions

Norsk Tindemuseum (The Norwegian Mountaineering Museum)

This museum, founded by legendary Norwegian mountaineer Arne Randers Heen and his wife, Bodil Roland, honors Norway's mountaineering heritage. The exhibits include Heen's climbing gear and stories of his incredible achievements, such as ascending Romsdalshorn, a 5,101-foot peak, 233 times —the last at age 85. The museum, now located in Norsk Tindesenter, Havnegata 2, Åndalsnes, also features interactive climbing experiences. Entry costs 140 NOK, and more details are available at tindesenteret.no.

Trollstigen

A scenic masterpiece, Trollstigen is one of Norway's most famous drives. Built by 100 workers over 20 summers starting in 1916, this road ascends through 11 hairpin bends, offering breathtaking views of peaks like Bispen (the Bishop), Kongen (the King), and Dronningen (the Queen). Open only in summer, Trollstigen typically opens in early June, as it did on June 9 in 2022. For more information, visit nasjonaleturistveger.no.

Utne

Nestled at the tip of a peninsula dividing Hardangerfjord and Sørfjord, Utne is a charming village and an ideal starting point for exploring the region. Visitors can discover historic farming communities, hike the rugged mountain slopes, or traverse nearby plateaus and glaciers. One of the most notable attractions is the Hardanger Folkemuseum, featuring medieval-era buildings and insights into Norway's cultural history.

Getting Here and Around

Ferries connect Utne to Kinsarvik via Route 13 and Kvanndal via Route 7. Alternatively, you can drive along scenic fjord roads from Odda.

Attractions

Hardanger Folkemuseum (Hardanger Folk Museum)
Dedicated to preserving local heritage, this museum offers an immersive glimpse into life in 19th-century Norway. The exhibits include traditional Hardingfele fiddles, Hardangerbunad attire, and intricate Hardangersaum embroidery. Visitors can explore historic houses and learn about cultural icons that influenced artists like Edvard Grieg. The museum, located at Museumsvegen 36, Vestland, charges 110 NOK for admission and is closed Saturday to Monday from September to April and on Mondays from May to August. Visit hardangerfolkemuseum.no or call 474-79-884 for details.

Utne Kyrkje (Utne Church)
Built in 1895 by renowned architect Peter Blix, Utne Church is a quaint wooden structure painted creamy white, accommodating up to 400 people. This historic parish, located at Fv 550 340, Vestland, reflects classic Norwegian ecclesiastical design. More information can be found at ullensvang.kyrkjer.no/Kyrkjelydane/Utne.

Olden

Situated at the eastern end of Nordfjord, Olden is one of the region's earliest tourist destinations, first attracting English fishermen seeking salmon in the 1860s. By the late 19th century, the area saw the rise of numerous hotels, accommodating the growing influx of visitors. Its most renowned attraction is the Briksdal Glacier, a branch of the Jostedal Glacier, located approximately 20 kilometers south of Olden. Accessible by car, bicycle, or on foot, the glacier can be visited from April to October.

Getting Here and Around

Olden is conveniently reached by car via Route 60 from Stryn and Loen.

Tours

Troll Shuttle

This fun and unique mode of transport takes visitors to the Briksdal Glacier and back in a 90-minute trip aboard open-air cars. The service operates from May to October, with reservations recommended. Starting at Briksdalbre in Vestland, further details are available at briksdal.com or by calling 57-87-68-05.

Attractions

Briksdal Glacier

An iconic arm of the Jostedal Glacier, Briksdal Glacier is a popular natural wonder located at the end of Oldedal Valley, about 20 kilometers south of Olden. Visitors can explore this breathtaking site by car, bicycle, or on foot between April and October. More information is available at Briksdalsbre Fjellstove, Vestland, through briksdal.no or by calling 57-87-68-05.

Olden Gamle Kyrkje (Olden Old Church)

Dating back to the 1700s, this charming white church occupies the site of a former stave church. Initially owned by a merchant, it was purchased by the village in the late 1800s. The church is located at Fv 724 169, Vestland.

Kinsarvik

Located by the Hardangerfjord, Kinsarvik offers stunning waterside views and access to some of Norway's finest hiking trails. This small village is a perfect starting point for outdoor enthusiasts eager to explore the region's natural beauty.

Getting Here and Around

Kinsarvik is easily accessible via Route 13, which connects it to Odda and Voss, although summer traffic can be heavy. Ferries from Utne provide direct access to the village, offering a scenic and convenient route.

Attractions

Husedalen
One of Norway's most scenic hikes, Husedalen takes you through a valley featuring four breathtaking waterfalls: Tveitafossen, Nykkjesøyfossen, Nyastølsfossen, and Søtefossen. The full hike, suitable for moderate hikers, takes about five to six hours, while visiting just the first waterfall takes approximately 90 minutes. Starting from Kinsarvik, hikers can follow the river and signs leading up the valley or drive to the power station for parking. EKinso Kraftverk, Vestland.

Mikkelparken
This family-friendly amusement park, named after a charming cartoon fox, features a water park, ziplines, playgrounds, and various activities for children. Located at Husevegen 6, Vestland, admission costs 389 NOK. The park operates from May to August and is closed from September to April. For hours during autumn, winter, and spring, call 53-67-13-13 or visit mikkelparken.no.

Eidfjord

Eidfjord, a small agricultural town, is known for its fjordhest (fjord horse), a breed integral to western Norway's farming heritage and prominently featured on the town's shield. Every spring, the Hingsteutstillinga (State Stallion Show) draws horse enthusiasts from across the region. With a population of around 6,000, Eidfjord offers an authentic farm experience. It is located near Hornindalsvatnet, northern Europe's deepest lake, while its sister village, Øvre Eidfjord, is home to the Hardangervidda Natursenter.

Getting Here and Around
Eidfjord, on the eastern edge of Hardangerfjord, serves as a gateway to the Hardangervidda Plateau. The journey from Bergen via Voss takes about 2½ hours, including crossing the impressive Hardanger Bridge. Follow E16 from

Bergen to Voss, then take Route 13 and turn onto Route 7 to reach Eidfjord.

Attractions

Kjeåsen Farm

Perched on steep fjordside cliffs, Kjeåsen Farm was once supplied via ropes and pulleys until a single-lane switchback road was constructed. Traffic alternates hourly, with uphill access during the first 30 minutes and downhill access during the last 30. Adventurous visitors can hike the 90-minute trail from the Sima power station parking lot, equipped with ropes and ladders. The panoramic view from the top is breathtaking, and tours may be available from the farm's owner. EOff Fv 103, Vestland.

Norsk Natursenter Hardanger

This interactive nature center in a stunning glass-and-steel building showcases exhibits on climate, nature, and the environment across three floors. A highlight is Ivo Caprino's 20-minute film Fjord Fjell Foss, offering a bird's-eye view of Norway. Located at Sæbøtunet 11, Vestland, the center charges an entry fee of 160 NOK and is closed from November to March. For more details, call 53-67-40-00 or visit norsknatursenter.no.

Vøringsfossen

Vøringsfossen, a 600-foot waterfall, has shaped the Måbødalen Valley over millennia. Accessible viewpoints along Route 7 between Eidfjord and Fossli provide stunning vistas. For a closer, misty view, take the half-hour hike to the base of the falls, though the trail is slippery even in dry conditions. Eidfjord tourist services at hardangerfjord.com can help plan your visit. ERte. 7, 20 minutes from Eidfjord, Vestland.

Geiranger fjord in western Norway

Balestrand

Balestrand, located along the Sognefjord, is famed for its scenic beauty and traditional wooden houses, which have inspired artists for over a century. Surrounded by three smaller fjord arms, the village offers a variety of outdoor activities for visitors.

Getting Here and Around

Balestrand is accessible by both boat and car. From Bergen, Voss, or Vik, drive to Vangsnes, take the car ferry to Dragsvik, and follow Route 55 to the village. Travelers from Oslo and Sogndal can take the Hella-to-Dragsvik car ferry before continuing on Route 55. Additionally, an express boat from Bergen stops directly in Balestrand.

Attractions

Nature Trail Kreklingen
This family-friendly and versatile trail offers hiking routes ranging from two to four hours, catering to both casual walkers and seasoned hikers. The trail features informational signs about the local flora and fauna, with a rewarding view of the village from its highest point. Start your journey at Kreklingevegen 3-5, Vestland.

St. Olaf's Church
Known as the English Church, this Anglican structure was the vision of Margaret Sophia Green, the daughter of an English minister who married a local resident. Built in the style of a stave church, it was completed in 1897 and stands as a unique landmark in the village. The church is located at Kong Beles Veg 35, Vestland.

Utsikten
A 40-minute drive from Balestrand along Gaularfjellet Tourist Route, this renowned viewpoint offers panoramic vistas of the surrounding valleys and mountains. The platform also provides a spectacular view of the winding hairpin turns below. Follow Route 13 and signs for Gaularfjellet to reach Utsikten. Visit nasjonaleturistveger.no for more details.

Flåm

Flåm is a picturesque village nestled at the end of the Sognefjord, Norway's longest fjord. Known for its stunning train journey to Myrdal, Flåm offers visitors a chance to enjoy breathtaking landscapes and explore the surrounding fjords. Staying overnight allows you to fully appreciate the tranquil beauty of the area once the day-trippers leave.

Getting Here and Around

From Voss, drive northeast on the E16 for about an hour, passing the Nærøyfjord, Norway's narrowest and most dramatic fjord. Buses connect Flåm with Voss (1 hour 15 minutes) and Bergen (3 hours). The Flåm railway station serves as the starting or ending point of the renowned Flåmsbana, which connects to Myrdal with further links to Voss, Geilo, Oslo, and Bergen. This train is as much about the views as it is about travel. For bus information, contact Nor-Way Bussekspress at 22-31-31-50 or visit www.nor-way.no. Visitor details are available through Norways Best, located at A-Feltvegen 11, Flåm, Vestland, reachable at 57-63-14-00 or www.norwaysbest.com.

Attractions

Flåmsbana (Flåm Railway)

The Flåm Railway is a 20 km (12 miles) journey that climbs 2,850 feet through steep mountain gorges, taking about an hour one way. Passing through 20 tunnels, this engineering marvel took 20 years to complete and is now one of Norway's most popular attractions, drawing over a million visitors annually. Trains operate year-round, with 8-10 round trips daily from mid-April to mid-October and four trips the rest of the year. Most tourists ride round-trip, returning shortly after arriving in Myrdal. Tickets are available for NOK 650 at Flåm Train Station, A-Feltvegen, Vestland. Visit www.norwaysbest.com for schedules and details.

Flåmsbana Museet

Located in the old station building just 300 feet from the current station, the Flåm Railway Museum offers an insightful look into the challenges faced while constructing the railway. The museum showcases this extraordinary engineering accomplishment and provides context to the journey. Admission is free, and the museum is located at Stasjonsvegen 8, Vestland. More information can be found at www.norwaysbest.com.

Restaurants

Ægir Bryggeri og Pub
This pub near the cruise port serves local dishes and award-winning beer, with mains averaging NKr300. Find it at A-Feltvegen 23, Vestland, 57-63-20-50, flamsbrygga.no.

Flåm Marina Restaurant
Enjoy local cuisine and fjord views, with mains around NKr250, at Vikjavegen 4, Vestland. Contact 57-63-35-55 or flammarina.no.

Flåmstova
This chalet-style eatery offers creative local dishes for NKr285. Located at A-Feltvegen 25, Vestland, 57-63-20-50, flamsbrygga.no.

Furukroa Kafé
This casual spot serves quick dishes, including soups, for NKr180. Visit A-Feltvegen 24, Vestland, 57-63-20-50, flamsbrygga.no.

Hotels

Flåm Marina and Apartments
Self-service apartments with fjord views start at NKr2000. Find them at Vikjavegen 4, Vestland, 57-63-35-55, flammarina.no.

Flåmsbrygga Hotel
This chalet-style hotel offers rooms with fjord views from NKr2990. Located at A-Feltvegen 25, Vestland, 57-63-20-50, flamsbrygga.no.

Fretheim Hotel
Elegant rooms start at NKr3100, with breakfast included. Visit Nedre Fretheimsvegen, Vestland, 57-63-63-00, fretheimhotel.no.

Heimly Pensjonat
Peaceful lodgings with fjord views start at NKr2790. Located at Vikjavegen 15, Vestland, 57-63-23-00, heimly.no.

Shopping

Flåm Store Exclusive
Shop unique gifts, including Aurland shoes, at A-Feltvegen 11, Vestland. Contact 57-63-14-00.

Activities

Fjord Cruise on the Nærøyfjord
This cruise through the UNESCO-listed Nærøyfjord offers stunning views of the fjord and mountains through glass-covered ships. The trip lasts 1.5 to 2.5 hours, depending on the vessel, and costs NKr540. Departures are from Flåm Pier, Vestland. Contact 57-63-14-00 or visit norwaysbest.com for more details.

eMobility Flåm
Explore the area in compact electric cars designed for two people, with pre-programmed GPS routes to ensure smooth navigation. Rentals start at NKr1250, available at Nedre Fretheim 15, Vestland. Contact 46-41-17-77 or visit emobflam.no for reservations.

Njord Kayaking
This company, located on Flåm Beach, offers guided kayaking adventures lasting from a few hours to several days, with courses for beginners. Reach them at 91-32-66-28 or visit seakayaknorway.com for schedules and bookings.

Brown Wooden House Near Mountain

Ålesund

Located between two brilliant blue fjords, Ålesund is one of Norway's largest fish-exporting harbors. Following a fire in 1904 that destroyed much of the town, the rapid rebuilding included the fusion of Art Nouveau and Viking architectural styles. The town, with its turrets, spires, and dragon motifs, stands as one of the world's few Art Nouveau cities. Walking tours can be arranged through the tourism office for a deeper exploration of this unique area.

Getting Here and Around

Vigra Airport, 15 km from the town center, connects Ålesund with major cities via SAS, Norwegian, WizzAir, and KLM, offering flights from Oslo, Bergen, Trondheim, Stavanger, Copenhagen, Kaunas, Gdansk, and Amsterdam. Airport buses take 25 minutes to the town, departing 10 minutes after arrivals. Ferries, including Hurtigruten and Havila, connect Ålesund to nearby islands and coastal locations. For road travel, Ålesund is accessible from Oslo (550 km via E6 and E136) and Bergen (390 km via E39), including two ferry crossings.

Visitor Information

For taxi services, contact Ålesund Taxi at 70-10-30-00 or visit alesund-taxi.no. For tourism inquiries, reach Destinasjon Ålesund og Sunnmøre at 70-16-34-30 or visit fjordnorway.com.

Attractions

Ålesunds Museum
The Ålesunds Museum offers a deep dive into the city's history, focusing on significant events such as the great fire of 1904 and the escape route used by the Norwegian Resistance during World War II. The museum also showcases local handicrafts in the folk-art style and features an Art Nouveau room dedicated to the town's architectural legacy. Located at Erasmus Rønnebergs gt. 16, Ålesund, the museum charges an entrance fee of NKr 75. For more details, visit walesunds.museum.no or call 70-16-48-42.

Alnes Fyr (Alnes Lighthouse)
Alnes Fyr, a striking red-and-white lighthouse on the Norwegian coast, offers spectacular views of the ocean. The site includes a gallery, a café open year-round, and an exhibition about the lighthouse's history. Located at Alnesgard, Godøya, Ålesund, admission is NKr 70. The lighthouse is closed on Mondays. For more information, visit walnesfyr.no or call 70-18-50-90.

Atlanterhavsparken (Atlantic Sea Park)
One of Scandinavia's largest aquariums, Atlanterhavsparken showcases the diverse marine life of the North Atlantic, including anglers, octopus, and lobster, with a special attraction for children being the Humboldt penguins. The park is located at Tueneset, Ålesund, 3 km west of town. Admission is NKr 225. To reach the park, take the Aquarium Bus ("Akvariebussen") from St. Olav's Plass, running from April to October. For more information, visit watlanterhavsparken.no or call 70-10-70-60.

Fiskerimuseet (Fisheries Museum)
The Fisheries Museum in Ålesund highlights the local fishing industry's history, especially focusing on those who stayed ashore to process the catch. The museum displays several exhibits, including one on tran (cod liver oil). Located at Molovegen 10, Ålesund, the entrance fee is NKr 70. The museum is closed from September to April, except on Saturdays. Visit wvitimusea.no or call 70-16-48-42 for more details.

Jugendstilsenteret (Art Nouveau Center)
Located in an architecturally captivating building, originally the Swan Pharmacy in 1907, the Jugendstilsenteret tells the story of Ålesund's Art Nouveau transformation after the 1904 fire. The center also includes the KUBE Art Museum. Admission is NKr 110, which covers both the Jugendstilsenteret and KUBE Art Museum. The center is closed on Mondays and operates from late August to late June. It is located at Apotekergata 16, Ålesund. For further details, visit wvitimusea.no.

Runde
Runde, a renowned bird rock in Norway, serves as a breeding ground for over 200 bird species, including puffins, gannets, and cormorants. The area is equipped with several observation points for wildlife enthusiasts. To get more information about the site, visit fjordnorway.com.

HKniven

For one of the best panoramic views of Ålesund, head to HKniven, a scenic viewpoint accessible by a drive up the city's mountain. This spot is popular for capturing stunning photos of the town, especially in the evening when the city lights create a sparkling vista. Visit Fjellstua Aksla, Ålesund for more details.

KUBE Art Museum

Located within the same complex as the Jugendstilsenteret, KUBE Art Museum is dedicated to contemporary Norwegian art. The museum promotes the work of emerging artists in a historic setting that once housed a branch of Norges Bank. Admission is NKr 110, which includes access to the Jugendstilsenteret. The museum is closed on Mondays from late August to late June. It is located at Apotekergata 16, Ålesund. For more information, visit wvitimusea.no.

Sunnmøre Museum

This open-air museum, located just five minutes from Ålesund at Museumsvegen 1, focuses on the history and traditions of coastal Norwegian life. The museum spans 50 acres and features 55 historic buildings, ranging from cow sheds to schoolhouses, offering a glimpse into the region's past. Admission is NKr 110, which includes access to the Medieval Museum. The museum is closed on Mondays from late August to late June. For more details, visit wvitimusea.no.

Restaurants

Egon Ålesund

Casual dining with a great selection of starters and vegetarian options. Average main: NKr 250. Løvenvoldgt. 8, Ålesund. Call 70-15-78-15 or visit wegon.no.

Fjellstua

Stunning mountain views and Norwegian dishes like salt cod and salmon. Average main: NKr 390. Fjellstua Aksla, Ålesund. Call 70-10-74-00 or visit wfjellstua.no.

Odda

Odda, situated by Hardangerfjord, serves as a convenient base for visiting

Folgefonna National Park and Trolltunga. The town offers a variety of cafés and restaurants for relaxation after exploring the nearby glaciers, waterfalls, and fjords. Odda also provides access to these remarkable sights, making it a popular stop for travelers seeking adventure and natural beauty.

Activities

Eidesnuten

This hike reaches a peak nearly 3,000 feet above sea level, offering spectacular views of Sandvinsvatnet and Sørfjord. The marked trail takes about 3-4 hours and includes steep sections, so a good level of fitness is required. The trailhead is near a small parking lot at Eidesåsen 100, Vestland.

Folgefonna National Park

Norway's third-largest glacier is in Folgefonna National Park, where visitors can kayak or hike on the glacier. Views of valleys and waterfalls from the top are stunning. The park has multiple entry points, with Odda and Rosendal being the main ones. Visit Skålafjæro 17, Vestland, or contact +53-48-42-80 for more details at wfolgefonna.info.

Trolltunga

This dramatic rock formation sits 3,600 feet above sea level, offering incredible views of the valley and fjord below. The 10-12 hour hike starts at Skjeggedal Carpark, Tyssedal, Vestland. Shuttle buses operate from Odda to P2, with additional shuttle service between P2 and P3 during the summer. For more info, visit www.hardangerfjord.com.

Hotels

Hardanger Hotel

Rooms from NKr1600, free parking, Wi-Fi, and breakfast. Eitrheimsveien 13, Vestland, +53-64-64-64, wwww.hardangerhotel.no.

Trolltunga Hotel

Rooms from NKr1880, breakfast, shuttle with guide. Vasstun 1, Vestland, +400-04-486, wwww.trolltungahotel.no.

Aurland

Aurland is a picturesque village nestled along the Aurlandsfjord, located just 10 minutes away from the bustling Flåm. Visitors come here to experience the tranquil atmosphere of fjord life, use the village as a starting point for the Aurlandsfjellet National Tourist Route, or explore the Stegastein Viewpoint, which offers one of the most breathtaking views in Norway. The viewpoint allows for a panoramic view of the fjords, providing an exceptional opportunity to fully appreciate the natural beauty of the region.

Getting Here and Around

Aurland can be easily accessed by car, situated about three hours' drive from Bergen along the E16 main road. The village is also reachable by boat, with both the express boat from Bergen and the fjord cruise between Flåm and Gudvangen making stops in Aurland.

Attractions

Aurland Shoe Factory

The Aurland Shoe Factory, located at EOdden 13, Vestland, is the only remaining shoe factory in Norway. It is believed to be the birthplace of the penny loafers, also known as "Weejuns," a name derived from the Norwegian term. Visitors can explore the history of this iconic shoe at the small museum inside the working factory. For more information, visit their website at aurlands.com or call +47 57 63 32 12.

Snow Road

The Snow Road, or Route 243, stretches from Aurland to Lærdal and is one of Norway's most scenic drives, particularly in the summer. The route gets its name due to the substantial snowfalls that close the mountain pass for much of the year. Learn more about this scenic drive at nasjonaleturistveger.no.

Stegastein

Just a 20-minute drive from Aurland, Stegastein is a renowned viewpoint offering panoramic vistas of the Aurlandsfjord extending all the way to Flåm. Though the road is challenging and winding, there are also buses available to take visitors to the viewpoint. More details are available at nasjonaleturistveger.no.

Vangen Kyrkje

Built in 1202, Vangen Kyrkje, also known as the Sogn Cathedral, is a stunning stone church located at Vangen 9, Vestland. It is the largest stone church in the area and a must-see for those interested in history and architecture.

Fjærland

Fjærland, a charming village nestled near the Jostedal Glacier, is known for its stunning green fjord, a unique color caused by the melting glaciers. This serene and distinctive water is one of Fjærland's main attractions, drawing visitors from around the world to admire the natural beauty of the area.

Getting Here and Around

Fjærland can be reached by car, with a 62 km (37 miles) drive south from Olden to Skei, which lies at the base of Lake Jølster. Route 5 passes under the glacier for over 6 km (4 miles) on the journey to Fjærland. In the summer, express boats operate between Flåm, Balestrand, and Fjærland, and a "glacier bus" travels from Fjærland to the Jostedal Glacier.

Sights

Fjærland Kyrkje (Fjærland Church)
The Fjærland Church, located at Mundalsvegen 6, Vestland, is a striking wooden church painted deep red. Built in 1861, it's a popular spot for photos, especially with the snow-capped mountain peaks as a stunning backdrop. For more information, visit sogndal.kyrkja.no.

Jostedal Glacier
Jostedal Glacier, Europe's largest glacier, stretches across the mountains between Sognefjord and Nordfjord. With over 100 known routes for crossing the glacier, it's essential to have a qualified guide if you wish to hike it. To reach Jostedalsbreen Glacier, take Route 55 from Solvorn, heading north to Route 604. Glacier Express buses are available during the summer months. Visit the Jostedalsbreen Glacier National Park Center for more details. For more information, go to jostedal.com. The Glacier Centre is closed from October to April.

Norsk Bremuseum (Norwegian Glacier Museum)
Located at Fjærlandsfjorden 13, Vestland, the Norsk Bremuseum is one of Norway's most innovative museums. Visitors can study glaciers up close by experimenting with ancient glacial ice, and they can also enjoy Ivo Caprino's unforgettable film on the Jostedal Glacier. The museum charges an entrance fee of NOK 140, and is closed from November to March. For more details, visit bre.museum.no.

Hellesylt

Hellesylt, a historic village that has been a popular trekking destination since the end of the last ice age, only began attracting tourists for overnight stays in 1875 when its first hotel was built. The village is known for its main attraction, a waterfall that sits uniquely between two bridges. Aside from the waterfall, there isn't much else to do in Hellesylt, but its charm lies in the natural beauty surrounding it.

Getting Here and Around

Hellesylt is most commonly visited by those on fjord cruises, as it is the final stop for many cruises. For travelers arriving by car, the village can be reached via Route 60.

Attractions

Hellesyltfossen
Hellesyltfossen, the waterfall in the heart of Hellesylt, is the village's main attraction. This waterfall is situated between two early 1900s bridges: Høge Bro and Hellesylt Bro. Visitors can admire the waterfall from both bridges, making it an iconic spot for photos. The waterfall is located along FV 60 in Hellesylt.

Peer Gynt Galleriet (Peer Gynt Gallery)
The Peer Gynt Gallery, located in Hellesylt, showcases wooden carvings inspired by Henrik Ibsen's play Peer Gynt. It is believed that Ibsen was inspired by the natural beauty surrounding Hellesylt. The gallery also serves as a visitor center, offering information about the local nature. For more details, visit peergyntgalleriet.no. The gallery is closed from early August to June.

Sunnylven Kirke
Sunnylven Kirke, situated near Hellesyltfossen, is a white wooden church completed in 1859. It is said to have been visited by Henrik Ibsen during his 1862 trip to Hellesylt. This church remains an important part of the village's history and can be visited while exploring the area.

Geiranger

Geiranger, a small village located at the end of the Geirangerfjord, has fewer than 300 year-round residents. However, during spring and summer, its population swells to around 5,000 as tourists flock here to experience the breathtaking views of the fjord. In the winter, the village becomes isolated due to snow on the mountain roads.

Getting Here and Around

The best way to explore the area's stunning landscapes is by boat or ferry. The ferry service between Geiranger and Hellesylt runs frequently during the summer, offering spectacular views of the waterfalls along Geirangerfjord. For those traveling by car, the most scenic route is a two-hour drive from Åndalsnes along Route 63, passing over Trollstigen (Troll's Ladder), and then continuing on the Ørneveien (Eagle's Road) to Geiranger, which has 11 hairpin turns.

Tours

eMobility
eMobility offers a unique way to explore the Geiranger area with small electric vehicles that follow preset routes, guided by GPS. Each vehicle accommodates two people. Located at Geirangervegen 2, Geirangerfjord, contact eMobility at +45 50 02 22 or visit emob.no.

Attractions

Flydalsjuvet
Flydalsjuvet is one of the most iconic viewpoints in Norway. A short 4 km (2.5 miles) drive from the center of Geiranger toward Grotli, this mountain plateau features two viewing platforms that offer spectacular views of Geirangerfjord. For more information, visit fjordnorway.com.

Geiranger Kyrkje (Geiranger Church)
Built in 1842, the octagonal Geiranger Church stands as the third church on the site. Designed by architect Hans Klipe, this wooden church offers a stunning view of the fjords. It's open only during the summer months. Located at Geirangerfjord, for more details, visit kyrkja.no/storfjorden.

Geiranger Skywalk Dalsnibba
The Geiranger Skywalk Dalsnibba, Europe's highest roadside viewpoint, offers a breathtaking view of Geiranger and its fjord. Visitors can drive for about 30 minutes along Nibbevegen from Geiranger to reach the viewpoint. Entrance costs NOK 270, with the toll road included in the fee. Visit dalsnibba.no for more details. Closed during winter.

Norsk Fjordsenter (Norwegian Fjord Centre)
The Norsk Fjordsenter is a comprehensive museum and visitor center, offering an introduction to the natural and cultural history of the Geirangerfjord, a UNESCO World Heritage site. Visitors can explore exhibits on the region's flora, fauna, and the technologies impacting the environment. The center is located at Gjørvahaugen 35, Geirangerfjord. Entrance is NOK 140, and it also offers a café and bookshop. For more details, visit fjordsenter.com. Electric car charging is available.

Ørnesvingen
Located along Ørnevegen (Eagle Road), Ørnesvingen is a viewpoint with one of the most dramatic views of Geiranger. This viewpoint is the perfect spot for capturing stunning photos of the fjord. It is located at FV 63, Geirangerfjord. For more information, visit nasjonaleturistveger.no.

Westerås Gard (Westerås Farm)
Westerås Farm, one of only three working farms in Geiranger, is situated just a few miles from the village. The farm offers spectacular views of the fjord and provides a simple restaurant in the barn, where visitors can enjoy local food. You can also stay in the farm's apartment or cabin. For more information, visit hanen.no/bedrift/625. The farm is closed from October to April.

Restaurants

Brasserie Posten
At Geirangervegen 4, enjoy local seafood and fjord views. Main dishes from

NKr 300. Contact +70 26 13 06 or visit brasserieposten.no. Closed Nov.–Mar.

Olebuda and Cafe Ole
Located in Gjørvahaugen, this spot serves local dishes. Main dishes from NKr 325. Contact +70 26 32 30 or visit Facebook. Closed Sept.–May (restaurant) and Oct.–Apr. (café).

Restaurant Julie
At Hotel Union, enjoy regional dishes with fjord views. Main dishes from NKr 300. Contact +70 26 83 00 or visit hotelunion.no.

Hotels

Grande Fjord Hotel
Located at Ørnevegen 200, with fjord views and free parking. Rooms from NKr 3550. Contact +70 26 94 90 or visit grandefjordhotel.com. Free breakfast included.

Hotel Union Geiranger
At Geirangervegen 101, offering buffet breakfast, free parking, and a car museum. Rooms from NKr 3190. Contact +70 26 83 00 or visit hotelunion.no. Free breakfast included.

Nightlife

The Lobby Bar
At Hotel Union, with panoramic fjord views. Contact +70 26 83 00 or visit hotelunion.no.

Shopping

Geiranger Gallery
Located at Maråkvegen 24, featuring local art and crafts. Open in summer.

Activities

Fjord Cruise Geiranger
This one-hour cruise through Geirangerfjord departs from Geiranger ferjekai. Book in advance as car spaces are limited. Ticket price: NKr 500. Contact +57

63 14 00 or visit norwaysbest.com. No tours in winter and spring.

Kristiansund

Kristiansund, once a major hub for timber and klippfisk (salted and sun-dried fish), grew into one of Norway's busiest ports by the 19th century. Today, Vågen, its lively harbor, offers a collection of historic boats. While World War II destroyed much of the town, Vågen remained intact, with several buildings still preserved.

Getting Here and Around

Kristiansund can be reached by Hurtigruten, with regular sailings making it an ideal arrival point by sea. The city's domestic airport also connects to Oslo and Bergen with multiple daily flights. However, driving from Oslo takes around 8 hours, and from Bergen, it's about 10 hours. While buses do connect most regions of Norway, they are infrequent.

Attractions

Grip Stavkyrkje (Grip Stave Church)
The Grip island is a quaint destination, highlighted by the red Grip Stave Church, perched at its highest point. Dating back to 1470, this church remains a symbol of the island's history. Although the fishing community largely vanished after World War II, locals return in the summer, joined by tourists. Ferries to Grip run at least once daily from Kristiansund between June and August. If the church is locked, locals can provide the key. To visit, contact Grip at +47 70 23 88 00 or visit www.visitgrip.com.

Kvalvik Fort
Kvalvik Fort, a well-preserved World War II military site, offers a fascinating glimpse into the past. Built by German forces, the fort housed 5,000 soldiers during its peak. Visitors can explore several bunkers, artillery guns, and a submarine. The site offers informative tours and exhibits, and its scenic location amidst wooded seaside hills draws locals who enjoy fishing and barbecues. Kvalvik Fort is located 13 km (8 miles) east of Kristiansund. To learn more, visit www.morotur.no/tur/Kvalvik-Fort.

Sundbåten

Kristiansund's ferry service, established in 1876, is the world's oldest public transportation still in operation. Ferries run two to three times an hour, offering scenic views of the city's layout and its distinctive colorful architecture. A round trip takes about 17 minutes. The service departs from Kirkelandet Sundbåtkai in Kristiansund. Tickets cost around NOK 40. For details, call +47 92 85 17 44 or visit www.sundbaten.no.

Restaurants

Bryggekanten Restaurant/Brasserie og Bache Bar

A casual waterfront spot serving seafood like crayfish, klippfisk, and grilled monkfish. Average main: NOK 370. Located at Storkaia 1, Kristiansund, open Tuesday to Saturday. Call +47 71 67 61 60 or visit www.fireb.no.

Sjøstjerna

Cozy restaurant offering bacalao, blandaball dumplings, and klippfisk, with Norwegian folk art decor. Average main: NOK 300. Located at Skolegata 8, Kristiansund. Call +47 71 67 87 78 or visit www.sjostjerna.no.

Loen

Loen, located near the Briksdal Glacier, offers easy access to some of Norway's most stunning hikes. Positioned on the eastern edge of the fjord, it provides spectacular scenery and serves as a gateway to the surrounding natural beauty.

Getting Here and Around
Loen is just a 10-minute drive from Olden, via Route 60.

Attractions

Loen Skylift

The Loen Skylift takes visitors to the top of Hoven Mountain, where they can enjoy breathtaking views of the fjord. Many opt to take the cable car up and walk down. At the summit, there is a viewpoint and a restaurant. The cable car ride costs NOK 555. Loen Skylift is located on Fv 60, Vestland, and operates from Wednesday to Sunday. It is closed on Mondays and Tuesdays in mid-October and from Monday to Thursday in November and January. For more details, visit www.loenskylift.com or call +47 57 87 59 00.

Lovatnet

Lovatnet, a stunning lake with striking green water from the melting glaciers, is known for its incredible photo opportunities. It's often considered one of the most beautiful lakes in Norway. Lovatnet is located along Fv 723 in Vestland.

The Austnesfjorden Fjord in Nordland, Norway

CHAPTER 8

TOP EXPERIENCE AND ADVENTURES

Top Attractions in Norway

Norway is a country of striking contrasts, blending vibrant cities like Oslo with dramatic landscapes of towering snow-covered peaks and deep fjords. Whether exploring the bustling capital or venturing into the wild, visitors can enjoy a variety of experiences, especially under the midnight sun or the mesmerizing northern lights.

Navigating the country is easy thanks to its efficient public transportation system, which doubles as a scenic experience. Trains and coastal ferries offer travelers the chance to admire Norway's landscapes while moving from place to place.

The country is home to a wealth of museums that offer a deep dive into its cultural history, from Viking heritage to maritime traditions, as well as art and entertainment. Each museum presents a unique aspect of Norwegian life and history, providing insight into the nation's evolution.

Norway's natural beauty is unparalleled, with its fjords, mountains, and glaciers forming the perfect backdrop for outdoor adventures. Many of these awe-inspiring locations are accessible to tourists, making it one of Europe's prime destinations for those seeking both adventure and breathtaking views.

Sognefjord
Sognefjord, Norway's largest fjord, stretches 204 kilometers inland from Skjolden and branches into numerous smaller fjords. Known as the "King of the Fjords," it spans nearly five kilometers at its widest point, with towering

cliffs reaching up to 1,307 meters. To fully experience its grandeur, boat tours and sightseeing cruises are the best options, with departures commonly from Bergen. These cruises are a full-day adventure, so plan accordingly. A must-see is the narrow Naeroyfjord, a 17-kilometer stretch where cliffs rise over 1,700 meters and are only 250 meters apart. Another highlight is Fjærland, home to Europe's largest glacier, Jostedalsbreen, and the Norwegian Glacier Museum, which explores the glacier's role and the region's climate change impact.

Website: www.sognefjord.no

Pulpit Rock (Preikestolen)

Pulpit Rock, located near Stavanger, is an iconic sight for active travelers. The trek involves a ferry ride, bus ride, and a two-hour hike uphill. Reaching the flat-topped cliff more than 600 meters above Lysefjord rewards adventurers with breathtaking panoramic views. Stavanger also boasts the Norwegian Canning Museum, located in a historic WWII-era cannery, showcasing the significance of sardine fishing. The 12th-century Stavanger Cathedral is another must-see, combining Romanesque, Baroque, and Gothic architectural styles.

Location: Rogaland, Norway

Lofoten Islands

The Lofoten Islands, off northwestern Norway's coast, are renowned for their mild weather despite being in the Arctic Circle. Visitors flock to the islands for hiking, kayaking, and exploring fishing villages. The islands are prime for northern lights sightings, as well as wildlife watching, where eagles, moose, and whales can be spotted. Svolvaer, the largest town in Lofoten, offers attractions such as the Lofoten War Memorial Museum, Magic Ice Lofoten, and the Lofoten Aquarium. Additionally, the Norwegian Fishing Village Museum and Lofoten Stockfish Museum in Å offer insight into the islands' fishing heritage.

Website: www.lofoten.info

Bygdoy Peninsula, Oslo

Located just four miles west of Oslo's center, Bygdoy Peninsula is home to several renowned museums and natural attractions. The Fram Museum showcases the polar voyages of the Fram ship, while the Kon-Tiki Museum focuses on Thor Heyerdahl's famous expeditions. The Norwegian Maritime Museum explores Norway's maritime history. The Center for Studies of

Holocaust and Religious Minorities is also located here, offering a deep reflection on Norway's past. Visitors can reach Bygdoy by car or public transport for a mix of cultural and scenic experiences.
Address: Bygdøynesveien 37, 0286 Oslo, Norway
Website: https://marmuseum.no/en

Bryggen Hanseatic Wharf, Bergen

Bryggen Hanseatic Wharf in Bergen is a vivid reminder of the city's history as a hub for Hanseatic trade. The area is home to brightly painted buildings, boutiques, and restaurants, as well as the Bryggen Museum. A must-visit is the Hanseatic Museum, housed in a 1704 merchant home, providing insight into life during the Middle Ages. While in Bergen, stop by Troldhaugen, the former home of composer Edvard Grieg, and explore the Open Air Market.
Location: Bryggen, 5003 Bergen, Norway
Website: https://stiftelsenbryggen.no

Tromsø's Arctic Museums

Tromsø, a prime spot for Arctic exploration, hosts several museums dedicated to the region's unique environment. Polaria offers exhibits on the northern lights, climate change, and Arctic wildlife, with an aquarium showcasing local marine life. The Polar Museum, focusing on Tromsø's history as a fishing community and polar research base, is another notable attraction.
Address: Hjalmar Johansens gate 12, 9296 Tromsø, Norway

Vigeland Sculpture Park, Oslo

Vigeland Sculpture Park in Oslo features 650 sculptures by Gustav Vigeland, arranged in five thematic groups. The most iconic is the fountain group, which portrays the cycle of human life, culminating in a 16-meter monolith. Located within Frogner Park, the park also houses the Vigeland Museum and Oslo City Museum. Visitors can enjoy the park's recreational facilities, including Norway's largest playground and a beautiful rose garden.
Address: Nobels gate 32, 0268 Oslo, Norway
Website: https://vigeland.museum.no/en

Akershus Fortress, Oslo

Akershus Fortress, built in 1299 by King Håkon V, offers a glimpse into Norway's medieval and Renaissance history. Set atop a promontory with stunning views of Oslofjord, the fortress grounds include the Museum of the Norwegian Resistance and the Norwegian Armed Forces Museum. Visitors can explore the fortress and enjoy public events, concerts, and ceremonies held on-site.

Address: 0150 Oslo, Norway

The Olympic Town of Lillehammer

Lillehammer, situated by Lake Mjøsa, is a year-round tourist destination. In summer, visit Maihaugen, an open-air museum with over 100 historic buildings, including a stave church and farmhouses. Peer Gynt's Cottage, dating from the early 1700s, is another notable site. During winter, Lillehammer transforms into a hub for snow-related activities. As the host city for the 1994 Winter Olympics, Lillehammer offers over 480 kilometers of Nordic ski trails, skating, curling, and sleigh rides.

Official site: http://en.lillehammer.com

Geirangerfjord

Geirangerfjord, located in Fjord Norway, is renowned for its breathtaking views and stands proudly on the UNESCO World Heritage list. This stunning fjord, which is part of the eastward continuation of the Sunnylvsfjord, offers panoramic vistas best viewed from Dalsnibba summit, 1,495 meters above the fjord. Travelers can enjoy the region through boat cruises or self-drive adventures, taking the famous Eagles' Road. The winding road, known for its 11 hairpin bends, offers dramatic views of Geirangerfjord below.

Atlantic Ocean Road

Stretching just over eight kilometers, the Atlantic Ocean Road (Atlanterhavsvegen) offers one of the world's most scenic coastal routes. This road, located between Eide and Averøy in Møre og Romsdal, connects small islands and is famous for its dramatic twists and turns. Visitors can explore fishing villages, wooden churches, and attractions like the Trolls' Church Cave. The area offers several tourism-focused services, including fishing excursions, resorts, and restaurants. More details can be found at www.nasjonaleturistveger.no/en.

Jotunheimen

Jotunheimen, Norway's largest Alpine region, spans 3,499 square kilometers and includes some of Scandinavia's highest mountains, including Galdhøpiggen, which rises over 2,438 meters. Known for its glaciers, rivers, lakes, and wildlife, Jotunheimen attracts adventurers for hiking, climbing, and skiing. To reach the summit of Galdhøpiggen, a four-hour climb with a guide is required.

For more challenging hikes, the Skagastølsbre glacier and Skagastølsbotn offer a steep, four-hour ascent. Jotunheimen Reiseliv, located in Lom, Norway, is your point of contact for guided tours and more information.

Marmorslottet

Less known but equally impressive is Marmorslottet (Marble Castle), located near Svartisen Glacier, less than an hour from Mo i Rana. Its deep blue waters, formed by glacial processes, make it a remarkable sight. The surrounding area's beauty and serenity make it a must-see for those visiting Svartisen.

Dovrefjell National Park

The Dovrefjell National Park in southeastern Norway, encompassing Dovre and Dovrefjell-Sunndalsfjella parks, spans 770 square miles and is famous for being home to wild musk oxen. These animals were introduced in the 20th century and can be seen up close on guided safaris. Visitors can also explore the park's rugged landscape and enjoy wildlife watching.

Gloppedalsura

Gloppedalsura, located in the Jæren region of Norway, is home to some of the largest boulders in northern Europe, remnants of a massive rockslide. The area, part of the Magma Geopark, offers a unique landscape that is as mesmerizing as it is educational.

Saltstraumen

Saltstraumen, located near Bodø, is home to the world's strongest tidal current. Every day, during high and low tides, massive amounts of seawater surge through a narrow strait, creating dramatic whirlpools. This natural phenomenon is a thrilling sight for visitors.

Jostedalsbreen

Jostedalsbreen, the largest glacier in Norway and continental Europe, spans almost 200 square miles. It features several branches, including the popular Briksdalsbreen, near Olden, where visitors can take guided "troll car" tours to explore the glacier's rugged beauty.

Vettisfossen

Vettisfossen, located in Jotunheimen National Park, is Europe's tallest unregulated free-falling waterfall, plummeting 900 feet. The hike to this majestic waterfall is a steep, 7.5-mile round trip through Utladalen. The trail is strenuous, but the reward is well worth the effort.

Hardangervidda

Hardangervidda, Europe's largest high-altitude plateau, covers almost 3,300 square miles and is home to Norway's largest national park. This area, with its vast tundra landscape, offers a range of activities, including hiking, wildlife watching, and exploring the unique flora and fauna that thrive in this region.

Stegastein Viewpoint

The Stegastein Viewpoint, designed by Todd Saunders and Tommie Wilhelmsen, extends 98 feet from the mountainside, offering a dramatic view of the surrounding fjords and mountains. Located 2,100 feet above sea level, this platform is a popular stop for travelers taking the Flåm Railway, providing one of the most stunning vistas in Norway.

Nidaros Cathedral

Located in Trondheim, Nidaros Cathedral holds the distinction of being the world's northernmost medieval cathedral. It was built between 1070 and 1300 and is of immense cultural and historical importance. The cathedral was originally constructed to honor King Olav II, later known as St. Olav, whose grave lies within the cathedral. It remains a prominent site for pilgrims and visitors alike.

Website: www.nidarosdomen.no
Address: Nidarosdomen, N-7013 Trondheim, Norway

Helleren i Jøssingfjord

Helleren i Jøssingfjord, located in southwestern Norway, is a historical site believed to have been inhabited since the 16th century. The site is uniquely sheltered beneath a massive 197-foot-long, 33-foot-high mountain overhang, providing a safe and expansive living space that has been preserved over centuries. This remarkable location offers a glimpse into the past and a stunning natural setting.

Location: Jøssingfjord, Norway

Arctic Cathedral

Tromsø's Arctic Cathedral, designed by the Norwegian architect Jan Inge Hovig in 1965, is one of the city's most iconic landmarks. The cathedral's distinctive triangular roof, which resembles either icebergs or northern Norwegian cod-drying racks, creates a striking silhouette in front of Mt. Storsteinen. The modern design and dramatic architecture make it a must-see for anyone visiting Tromsø.

Address: Tromsø, Norway

Loen Skylift

Loen Skylift is one of Norway's most thrilling cable car experiences, offering an exhilarating ascent up Mt. Hoven. The steepest cable car line in the country, it reaches an elevation of 3,600 feet in just five minutes, providing breathtaking views of the surrounding landscapes. Despite its pricey ticket, it is a major attraction for tourists seeking adventure and stunning panoramic vistas.

Address: Loen, Norway

Website: www.loenskylift.no

Atlantic Ocean Road Bridges

The Atlantic Ocean Road, a 5-mile stretch of Norwegian Road 64, is renowned for its dramatic bridges and stunning views. This remarkable engineering feat connects the mainland with Averøy Island, and features eight bridges, including the Storseisundbrua, which is the longest and highest. The Atlantic Ocean Road is often listed as one of the world's best road trips, offering an unforgettable drive along the rugged Norwegian coastline.

Location: Averøy Island, Norway

Northern Lights Cathedral

Completed in 2013, the Northern Lights Cathedral in Alta is an architectural masterpiece. Designed by the Norwegian firm LINK, it features a modern design that evokes the beauty of the aurora borealis. The cathedral is illuminated by light installations that reflect the vibrant colors of the northern lights, making it a captivating experience both inside and out.

Address: Alta, Norway

Under Restaurant

Under, located in Lindesnes, is Europe's first subaquatic restaurant, offering diners a unique opportunity to enjoy fine Norwegian cuisine while observing the marine life through panoramic windows. The restaurant's innovative design and exceptional dining experience make it one of Norway's most sought-after culinary destinations.

Address: Lindesnes, Norway

Website: www.under.no

Snøhetta Viewpoint

The Snøhetta Viewpoint, part of the Norwegian Wild Reindeer Centre Pavilion, offers breathtaking views of Mt. Snøhetta and the surrounding Dovrefjell-Sunndalsfjella National Park. The building is an architectural gem and is

accessible via a hiking trail from the Snøhetta parking lot or the nearby train station at Hjerkinn. Open from June to mid-October, it's a popular spot for nature lovers and hikers.
Website: www.dovrefjell.com
Location: Dovrefjell, Norway

Hopperstad Stave Church
Hopperstad Stave Church, constructed in 1130, is one of Norway's oldest and most important stave churches. The church was restored in the late 19th century by architect Peter Andreas Blix, who drew inspiration from the Borgund Stave Church. It stands as a remarkable example of medieval wooden architecture in Norway and remains a popular tourist destination.
Address: Hopperstad, Norway
Must-Sees for Art Lovers in Oslo

Munch Museum
The Munch Museum in Oslo is dedicated entirely to the works of Edvard Munch, one of Norway's most famous painters. Best known for his iconic painting The Scream, Munch's expressive and emotional style is celebrated in over 1,200 works in the museum's collection. Stolen in 2004 and later recovered, The Scream remains a highlight of the museum.
Website: www.munchmuseet.no
Address: Oslo, Norway

Kragstøtten
Kragstøtten is a viewpoint that offers stunning panoramic views of Oslo, with a statue commemorating Hans Hagerup Krag, a 19th-century Norwegian road commissioner. Krag is celebrated for developing the roads in the Holmenkollen district, which is now home to the famous ski jump. The statue and the viewpoint are key landmarks in Oslo's scenic landscape.
Location: Holmenkollen, Oslo, Norway

Peer Gynt Sculpture Park
The Peer Gynt Sculpture Park in northeastern Oslo is dedicated to the works of playwright Henrik Ibsen. The 20 sculptures in the park depict scenes from Ibsen's Peer Gynt, and they are the creations of contemporary artists. The park offers a blend of nature and art, making it a peaceful and inspiring place to visit.
Location: Oslo, Norway

Vigelandsparken

Vigelandsparken, also known as Frogner Park, is home to the impressive works of local sculptor Gustav Vigeland. Featuring over 200 sculptures in granite and bronze, the park is one of Oslo's most famous attractions. The centerpiece of the park is the 46-foot monolith, which represents all stages of life, from birth to death.
Address: Oslo, Norway

Ekeberg Sculpture Park

Nestled in the hills east of Oslo, Ekeberg Sculpture Park is a beautiful combination of art and nature. The park is home to more than 40 sculptures, which are carefully positioned to blend with the surrounding landscape, offering breathtaking views of the city and fjord. It's a serene spot to experience contemporary art in a natural setting.
Location: Oslo, Norway

Tjuvholmen Sculpture Park

Located along Oslo's picturesque fjord, the Tjuvholmen Sculpture Park features contemporary works by several renowned artists. Designed by architect Renzo Piano, the park is part of the vibrant Tjuvholmen neighborhood, which is home to art galleries and museums. The park is a beautiful way to explore Oslo's thriving art scene.
Location: Oslo, Norway

Vippa

Vippa, an international street food court located by the Vippetangen port, offers an array of culinary delights from around the world. With dishes representing the diverse cultures of Norway, Eritrea, Syria, and China, Vippa is a place to sample the world's flavors while enjoying a vibrant atmosphere.
Location: Oslo, Norway

The National Museum

The National Museum in Oslo is the country's premier public collection for art, architecture, and design. It showcases works from a range of historical periods, from ancient times to the modern day, offering a comprehensive look at the evolution of art and design in Norway and beyond.
Website: www.nasjonalmuseet.no
Address: Oslo, Norway

The Tiger

Oslo's central train station is home to a 15-foot-long bronze statue of a tiger, which has become a symbol of the city. Known as The Tiger, this iconic sculpture commemorates Oslo's 1,000-year anniversary and has become one of the most photographed landmarks in the capital.
Location: Oslo, Norway

Holmenkollen Troll

The Holmenkollen Troll is a 23-foot-tall concrete sculpture located in the forests of the Holmenkollen district. This whimsical figure is easy to spot during visits to the area, adding a touch of fantasy to the outdoor experience.
Location: Oslo, Norway

Norway fjord camping landscape

Outdoor Activities

Scenic Rail Journeys Across Norway
Norway's rail system, extending over 3,218 kilometers, offers an unparalleled way to explore the country's breathtaking landscapes. Despite the mountainous terrain, the network connects a variety of scenic routes, cutting through over 775 tunnels and crossing more than 3,000 bridges. For the most scenic journeys, start in Oslo with the Bergen Railway, which traverses the Hardangervidda plateau. Other notable lines include the Dovre Railway, connecting Oslo to Trondheim, and the Rauma Railway, running from Dombås to Åndalsnes. The Flåm Railway, known for being the steepest in the world, is another unforgettable experience. Norway's rail offerings also extend to historic steam train rides, gourmet excursions, and pedal-powered rail tricycles for those seeking unique adventures on unused tracks.

Chasing the Northern Lights
The Northern Lights, one of the world's most captivating natural phenomena, can be seen in the dark, remote regions of Norway. This dazzling display of green and pink hues occurs when charged particles collide with Earth's atmosphere. The best time to witness this spectacular event is between October and February, when the sky is clearest and the nights longest. Norway's pristine, light-pollution-free areas offer optimal views of this mesmerizing light show.

Driving to Nordkapp
A visit to Nordkapp, the northernmost point of mainland Europe, is an essential journey for those with a motorhome or camper. The dramatic meeting point of the Arctic Ocean and sky offers a surreal experience year-round. In summer, you can marvel at the midnight sun, while winter brings the chance to witness the magical Northern Lights. Nordkapp stands as a year-round must-see, offering unparalleled natural beauty and solitude.

Wild Swimming in Glacial Waters
For an invigorating, truly refreshing experience, dive into the crystal-clear waters of one of Norway's many glacial lakes. These pristine bodies of water, often nestled among towering snow-capped peaks, provide a one-of-a-kind opportunity to connect with nature while swimming in some of the world's purest waters. Lovatnet, for example, is a glacial lake so cold it literally takes your breath away. Swimming beneath the glacier is a magical experience that

should not be missed.

Kayaking Through Geirangerfjord

Geirangerfjord, a UNESCO World Heritage Site, offers one of Norway's most stunning landscapes, with towering cliffs and beautiful waterfalls. Kayaking through this majestic fjord provides a unique, up-close view of the natural wonders it holds. Whether navigating solo in inflatable kayaks or joining a guided tour, you'll get an unforgettable view of Geirangerfjord's iconic Seven Sisters Waterfall as it cascades down the cliffs.

Visiting Saltstraumen

For those seeking natural phenomena, Saltstraumen, near Bodø, is the place to witness the world's strongest tidal current. This powerful force of nature is a great location for fishing and offers an incredible spectacle for anyone nearby. It's a perfect destination for those intrigued by the raw power of nature.

Taking the Polar Plunge

For those with an adventurous spirit, plunging into the frigid Arctic waters is an exhilarating experience. The polar plunge is not for the faint of heart but offers a true test of bravery and a chance to immerse yourself in Norway's rugged Arctic environment. The icy waters are invigorating and provide a refreshing connection to the region's natural elements.

Sleeping in an Ice Igloo

While many experiences in Norway are budget-friendly, staying in an ice igloo is a luxurious exception. Sleeping surrounded by the breathtaking winter landscape in an ice igloo is an otherworldly experience. Wrapped in a thermal sleeping bag, you'll spend the night beneath the stars, all while witnessing the Northern Lights dancing above in the sky. It's an unforgettable way to experience Norway's cold beauty.

Cozy Cabin Stay in the Wilderness

For a peaceful retreat into nature, a stay in a remote cabin in the Norwegian wilderness is an ideal way to unwind. Many cabins are accessible for free, making them an affordable option for those seeking tranquility. Although some may feel eerie, these cabins offer a genuine escape, providing a perfect setting for quiet reflection and connecting with the surrounding wilderness.

Hiking Behind a Waterfall

Norway's landscape is home to numerous breathtaking waterfalls, and one of the most exhilarating ways to experience them is by hiking behind the cascading waters. A particularly rewarding hike is to Storsæterfossen in Geiranger. After a 40-minute climb to a scenic viewpoint, you can descend to walk behind the waterfall itself. As you stand in the mist and feel the immense force of the water, you'll have a firsthand experience of nature's power. For a quieter hike, try to arrive early to avoid the crowds from nearby cruise ships.

Sauna Experience with Fjord Views

Experience the ultimate in relaxation by unwinding in a traditional Norwegian sauna, all while enjoying panoramic views of a fjord. Sauna culture is deeply embedded in Norwegian tradition, and this combination of wellness and nature offers an enriching experience. One of the best spots is Fjærland, where a sauna situated on a glacial lake provides the perfect tranquil backdrop. It's an ideal way to disconnect, refresh, and enjoy Norway's majestic surroundings.

Hike to Segla Summit in Senja

Senja, known for its rugged landscapes, offers one of the most exhilarating hikes to Segla, a mountain famous for its sail-like peak. The trail is challenging but rewards adventurers with breathtaking views from the summit. The hike is perfect for those seeking a physical challenge paired with unmatched natural beauty, offering panoramic vistas of Norway's untamed wilderness.

Exploring Trollkirka Cave System

While Norway is renowned for its iconic hikes, such as Pulpit Rock and Trolltunga, Trollkirka, a lesser-known gem, is a must for those seeking something unique. After a one-hour hike, you'll reach a stunning cave system, where you can explore independently. Inside, discover a magnificent waterfall, earning the cave its nickname, the Troll's Church. This eerie and fascinating hike offers a truly otherworldly experience, perfect for nature enthusiasts.

Tip: Be sure to bring a flashlight as the caves are completely dark inside.

Spotting Moose at the Observation Tower

For those fascinated by wildlife, Norway offers an exceptional opportunity to observe moose in their natural environment from a specially designed observation tower. Witnessing these majestic creatures up close is a unique experience that showcases Norway's rich wildlife. If visiting Norway's observation towers isn't within your budget, head across the border to Sweden to visit Dalsands Mosse Ranch for an alternative wildlife experience.

Booktown Fjærland: A Literary Escape

Fjærland, a picturesque town nestled between mountains and glaciers, is a haven for book lovers. Known as Booktown, this charming village features numerous independent bookstores, making it a paradise for bibliophiles. The serene setting provides an ideal backdrop for leisurely exploring the many bookstores while enjoying the surrounding natural beauty.

UFO Spotting in Hessdalen

In 1981, mysterious lights were first spotted in the Hessdalen Valley in Trøndelag, sparking intrigue among researchers and enthusiasts. Today, Hessdalen remains a hotspot for UFO sightings, drawing visitors from all over the world to observe these phenomena. Stay at the Hessdalen UFO cabin or camp to potentially experience these strange occurrences for yourself.

Ride Norway's Longest Toboggan Run

While Norway is famous for its skiing, there's also plenty of fun to be had without skis. In Loen, Fjord Norway, you can take the Skylift to the top of a mountain and race down the world's longest toboggan run, stretching for 7 kilometers. It's a thrilling ride down to the fjord, offering excitement for both kids and adults—just be ready for a fast-paced descent!

Meet Modern-Day Vikings in Njardarheimr

Viking heritage is alive and well in Njardarheimr, a town where history and tradition meet the present. In this Viking settlement, the residents live and work just as their ancestors did, with no actors or costumes—these are real Vikings who have incorporated authentic details into their modern lives. Explore the fascinating Viking history in this living museum, where you can learn about their crafts, traditions, and way of life.

Sea Eagle Safari Adventure

The majestic sea eagle, known for its speed and impressive size, is a rare sight, often only visible from a distance. However, on a sea eagle safari in Northwest Norway, you may have the chance to see these magnificent birds up close as they approach boats in search of food. Stay alert and you might catch a fleeting glimpse of these powerful creatures as they soar through the sky.

Spend Time with a Sami Reindeer Herder
For a truly unique cultural experience, spend the day with a Sami reindeer herder and learn about the traditional lifestyle of the indigenous Sami people. This rare opportunity allows you to immerse yourself in their world and gain firsthand knowledge of their customs, as well as the importance of reindeer herding to their way of life. It's a deep dive into an ancient culture that has thrived in Norway's rugged Arctic regions.

A Visit to Hell (Norway)
Contrary to what the name might suggest, Hell is a real town in Norway! Situated near Trondheim, Hell is an amusing and popular stop for travelers seeking a fun photo op at the old train station. Located close to Trondheim Airport Værnes, Hell is also a convenient stop if you're exploring the Trøndelag region. Just remember to dress warmly, especially during the winter months when temperatures can dip, making it quite literally a "cold day in Hell."

Girl standing on top of the fjord Eidfjord in Norway

CHAPTER 9

ESSENTIAL TRAVEL INFORMATION

Currency

The official currency is the Norwegian Krone (NOK), abbreviated as "kr". Banknotes come in denominations of 50, 100, 200, 500, and 1000 NOK, while coins include 1, 5, 10, and 20 NOK.

Public Holidays

Public holidays in Norway often close offices, banks, post offices, and some shops, especially outside major cities.
- New Year's Day (January 1)
- Maundy Thursday (Thursday before Easter)
- Good Friday (Friday before Easter)
- Easter Sunday and Monday (dates vary)
- Labour Day (May 1)
- Constitution Day (May 17)
- Ascension Day (40 days after Easter)
- Whit Monday (Monday after Pentecost)
- Christmas Day (December 25)
- Boxing Day (December 26)

On these days, essential services remain operational, but public transport may run on reduced schedules.

Time Zone
Norway operates on Central European Time (CET), which is UTC+1. During daylight saving time (March to October), the clock moves to UTC+2.

Language
Norwegian is the official language, with two written forms: Bokmål and Nynorsk. English is widely spoken, especially in cities, making communication relatively easy for travelers.

Healthcare
Healthcare in Norway is of high quality. EU/EEA citizens can use their European Health Insurance Card (EHIC) for medical treatment. Travelers from other countries are advised to have comprehensive travel insurance. Pharmacies ("Apotek") are widely available for minor ailments and prescriptions.

Electricity
Norway uses 230V electricity with a frequency of 50Hz. The standard plug type is the European two-pin plug (Type C and F).

WiFi and Internet Access
WiFi is widely available in hotels, cafes, restaurants, and public areas, often free of charge. Mobile data coverage is excellent, even in remote areas.

Visas
Norway is part of the Schengen Area. Citizens of EU/EEA countries do not need a visa. Other nationalities may require a short-stay Schengen visa for visits up to 90 days. Always check visa requirements before traveling.

Money

- ATMs: ATMs (Minibank) are widespread and accept major cards such as Visa, Mastercard, and American Express.
- Changing Money: Currency exchange services are available at airports, banks, and major cities.
- Credit Cards: Credit and debit cards are widely accepted for payments, even for small transactions.
- Major Banks: DNB, Nordea, and SpareBank are prominent banks with ATMs across the country.

Cell Phones

Norway has a robust mobile network with excellent coverage. Travelers can use their phones with roaming services or purchase a local SIM card from providers like Telenor, Telia, or Ice. SIM cards are available at airports, electronic stores, and supermarkets, requiring an ID for activation.

Plugs and Adaptors
Norway uses Type C and F plugs. Travelers from countries with different plug types should bring an adaptor.

Tipping

Tipping is not mandatory but appreciated for good service:
- Airport & Hotel Parking Attendants 10-20 NOK.
- Bartenders: Round up the bill.
- Hotel Maids: 10-20 NOK per day.
- Parking Valets: 10-20 NOK.
- Restaurant Servers: 5-10% of the bill for excellent service.
- Taxi Drivers: Round up the fare to the nearest 10 NOK.

Opening Hours

- Restaurants: Lunch service (11:00-15:00), dinner (17:00-22:00).
- Bars: Open from 15:00-01:00, with extended hours on weekends.
- Shops: Monday-Friday (09:00-18:00), Saturday (10:00-16:00), closed on Sundays except for convenience stores.
- Banks: Monday-Friday (09:00-15:00), some extended hours in cities.
- Post Offices: Monday-Friday (09:00-17:00), reduced hours on Saturdays.
- Hotels: Reception is usually open 24/7.

Other Important Information

Norway is exceptionally safe, but travelers should still exercise standard precautions. Public transport is reliable and efficient, with trains, buses, and ferries connecting cities and rural areas. Additionally, tap water is safe to drink, reducing the need for bottled water. Always carry suitable clothing for sudden weather changes, especially in mountainous or coastal regions.

Travel Itinerary

A 5-Day Itinerary

Western Norway is renowned for its spectacular fjords, and with five days to spare, you can experience some of the most breathtaking landscapes the region has to offer. Arrive at Bergen Airport (BGO) and depart from the same airport to complete your journey.

Day 1: Explore Bergen
Begin your journey by flying into Bergen Airport and picking up your pre-booked rental car. On your way into the city, stop by Fana to visit the Fantoft Stave Church, one of only 28 remaining in Norway. Although it was destroyed by fire in 1992, it has been carefully rebuilt to replicate its original design. Upon arrival in Bergen, park your car at the Hurtigruten Terminal before exploring the city on foot. The Fisketorget fish market and Bryggen, the historic wharf lined with traditional wooden buildings, offer a glimpse into Bergen's maritime past. If time permits, visit Bergenhus Festing, one of the oldest fortresses in Norway, or take the Fløibanen funicular for stunning views of the city from Mt. Fløyen. The Hurtigruten departs in the evening, so return to the ship early for dinner.

Logistics: 11 miles from the airport (20 minutes by car). Bergen's city center is easily walkable.

Day 2: Ålesund and Geiranger
After a restful night aboard the Hurtigruten, enjoy a hearty breakfast before arriving in Ålesund. The city is known for its well-preserved Art Nouveau architecture, a result of the fire that devastated Ålesund in 1904. Visit the Art Nouveau Center to learn about this history and the city's unique architecture. For nature lovers, a hike up Mt. Aksla provides panoramic views of Ålesund and the surrounding fjords. In the afternoon, continue your drive to Geiranger, passing by Trollstigen, a serpentine mountain road famous for its beauty. On the way, stop at Stigfossen waterfall, a popular photo spot. Once in Geiranger, visit the Flydalsjuvet viewpoint for a stunning overlook of the village.

Logistics: 250-mile Hurtigruten journey from Bergen to Ålesund (12 hours by boat); 65 miles from Ålesund to Geiranger (3 hours by car).

Day 3: Geirangerfjord, Loen, and Solvorn

Start the day with a scenic ferry ride from Geiranger to Hellesylt. This is the best way to appreciate the beauty of Geirangerfjord and the iconic Seven Sisters waterfall. From Hellesylt, drive to Loen, where you'll find the Loen Skylift, a cable car that takes you to the top of Mt. Hoven in just five minutes. This is one of the steepest cable cars in the world, offering a thrilling ride with panoramic views of Jostedalsbreen National Park. From the summit, you can explore hiking trails before heading toward Sognefjord. If possible, stay overnight at Walaker Hotel in Solvorn, a charming and historic establishment.

Logistics: 50 miles from Geiranger to Hellesylt (1 hour by ferry); 38 miles from Hellesylt to Loen (1 hour by car); 91 miles from Loen to Solvorn (2 hours by car).

Day 4: Lærdal, Aurland, and Eidfjord

Take the ferry from Mannheller to Fodnes, and then drive to Lærdal, a village known for its well-preserved 18th- and 19th-century wooden houses. Close by, you'll find Borgund Stave Church, built in 1180 and still standing as a testament to Norway's medieval religious architecture. After exploring the church, drive through the Lærdalstunnel, one of the world's longest road tunnels, to reach Aurland. While in Aurland, don't miss Stegastein, a viewing platform offering awe-inspiring views of Aurlandsfjord. Continue to Eidfjord, passing the Skjervsfossen waterfall, located just a short drive from the main road between Voss and Granvin.

Logistics: 2 miles from Mannheller to Fodnes (30 minutes by ferry); 23 miles from Fodnes to Borgund (30 minutes by car); 29 miles from Borgund to Aurland (45 minutes by car); 78 miles from Aurland to Eidfjord (2 hours by car).

Day 5: Return to Bergen

On your final day, make your way back to Bergen, taking the scenic Norwegian Tourist Route via Steinsdalsfossen waterfall. A walking path leads you behind the falls, offering a unique perspective of the natural beauty surrounding you.

Logistics: 94 miles from Eidfjord to Bergen Airport (3 hours by car).

Travel Tips
This itinerary is best suited for late spring to early autumn due to limited daylight in the winter months and possible road closures. Especially during the summer, it's recommended to book accommodations, car rentals, and ferry crossings in advance. For the Hurtigruten journey, reservations can only be made via phone or through a travel agency. Online booking is available exclusively on the official Norwegian website.

Exploring Northern Norway in Seven Days

Northern Norway, renowned for its winter northern lights and summer hikes under the midnight sun, offers travelers an unforgettable experience. This seven-day itinerary is designed to combine city exploration with a scenic road trip through the Arctic Circle, highlighting the Lofoten Islands and surrounding natural wonders.

Day 1: Arrival in Bodø
Start your adventure by flying into Bodø, where you can pick up your pre-arranged rental car. Begin your exploration with a hike up the Sherpa Staircase to Mt. Keiservarden for panoramic views of the city and its surroundings. For those preferring a more relaxed start, visit the Norwegian Aviation Museum to delve into the nation's history in aviation. In the evening, wander around Bodø's city center to enjoy colorful murals and treat yourself to exquisite chocolate pralines at Craig Alibone. The city center is walkable, and parking is available next to the Norwegian Aviation Museum and at Rønvikfjellet for the hike to Keiservarden.

Day 2: Exploring Bodø's Surroundings
On your second day, venture outside the city. Start with a visit to Mjelle, a serene sandy beach north of Bodø, perfect in any weather. Continue your journey to Kjerringøy, a peninsula near Sjunkhatten National Park, and explore the famous Kjerringøy Trading Post, a historical site central to the region's fish trading history since the 19th century.

Day 3: Saltstraumen and Travel to Svolvær
Make your way to Saltstraumen, home to one of the world's strongest tidal currents. When the tides change, the powerful whirlpools create a breathtaking spectacle. From there, head towards the Lofoten Islands. You can take your rental car on the Hurtigruten cruise to Svolvær (6 hours), or opt

for the express boat (3 hours) and rent another car upon arrival in Svolvær.

Day 4: Henningsvær and Nusfjord
Begin your exploration of the Lofoten Islands with a visit to Henningsvær, a charming village known for its coastal soccer field and the Kaviar Factory contemporary art museum. Continuing south, stop by the Lofotr Viking Museum to immerse yourself in Viking history and learn about their journeys to Iceland and Greenland. Afterward, head to Unstad Beach, the prime spot for local surfers. Finish the day in Nusfjord, a traditional fishing village that exudes authentic Norwegian charm.

Day 5: Scenic Views at Reine
Your fifth day in the Lofoten Islands will offer some of the most spectacular scenery. Start with a visit to Ramberg Beach, famous for its half-mile-long stretch of sand and stunning views. Enjoy traditional Norwegian cuisine for lunch at Ramberg Gjestegård. Later, drive to Reine, often considered the most photographed village in the Lofoten Islands, and take in the breathtaking landscapes surrounding this iconic location.

Day 6: Hike to Trolldalsvatnet and Visit Å
While the Reinebringen trail is popular, consider taking the Trolldalsvatnet trail for a more peaceful hike. This 5-mile, easy route offers stunning views of the mountains and leads to a picturesque lake. Afterward, explore the village of Å before driving back to Svolvær in the afternoon to return your rental car. Depending on your schedule, you can take the express boat the next morning or opt for the Hurtigruten cruise back to Bodø.

Day 7: Return to Bodø
On your final day, take the express boat from Svolvær to Bodø. Catch your afternoon flight back home, concluding your immersive journey through Northern Norway.

This itinerary offers a comprehensive experience of Northern Norway's natural beauty, with a blend of scenic hikes, historic sites, and unique cultural destinations.

A 6-Day Journey Through Norway

This iconic route from Oslo to Bergen, introduced in the 1960s by Norway's national rail service, offers one of the most scenic train-and-ferry journeys in the world. While the trip can be completed in a single day, taking more time allows you to fully appreciate the breathtaking landscapes along the way. Ideal for independent travelers, the journey is a perfect blend of dramatic fjords, mountain villages, and vibrant cities.

Days 1 and 2: Exploring Oslo

Arrive in Oslo, the perfect starting point for your adventure. The compact city is easy to navigate, and its mix of modern and historic attractions ensures an enriching experience. On the first day, begin with a visit to the Opera House's rooftop, offering spectacular views of the harbor. From there, head to the newly renovated Nasjonalmuseet and the Munchmuseet to discover Norway's rich artistic heritage. In the afternoon, wander through the lively waterfront areas of Aker Brygge and Tjuvholmen, filled with dining options. Day two takes you to the impressive Akershus Festning fortress and the Royal Palace, Slottet. Afterwards, explore the Bygdøy peninsula, home to museums like the Norsk Folkemuseum and the Viking Ship Museum. For dinner, visit Grünerløkka, a trendy area favored by locals.

Oslo's city center is pedestrian-friendly, and the Bygdøy peninsula is accessible by ferry or bus.

Day 3: Oslo to Flåm

Start early and take the Bergen line train to Myrdal. At Myrdal station, transfer to the Flåmsbana railway, a scenic route that descends through dramatic cliffs and waterfalls. This 12-mile journey to Flåm takes about an hour and offers incredible views. Upon arrival in Flåm, spend the afternoon relaxing in a café, shopping for souvenirs, or visiting the Flåmsbanemuseet to learn about the railway's construction. Spend the night in Flåm or nearby villages.

Flåm is small and walkable, making it easy to explore on foot.

Day 4: Flåm to Voss

Your day begins with a boat trip through Aurlandsfjord, entering the UNESCO-listed Nærøyfjord, Europe's narrowest fjord. This two-hour cruise offers views of majestic cliffs and serene waters. At Gudvangen, transfer to a bus for a one-hour ride along the winding Stalheimskleivane Road to Voss. If possible, stay at the historic Stalheim Hotel, located about 22 miles outside Voss.

Voss can be explored on foot.

Days 5 and 6: Discovering Bergen

From Voss, a one-hour train ride brings you to Bergen. Upon arrival, check into your hotel and head to Bryggen, the UNESCO-listed historic wharf, to explore some of Bergen's oldest buildings. Afterward, stroll through the fish market for local delicacies. On day six, take the Fløibanen funicular to the summit of Mt. Fløyen for panoramic views of the city and surrounding fjords. If time permits, visit the Edvard Grieg Museum south of the city, dedicated to the famous composer. From Bergen, you can either return to Oslo by train or plane or catch a flight home directly from Bergen.

Bergen's city center is also walkable and easy to explore on foot.

Travel Tips

Booking train and ferry tickets independently, especially during peak summer months, can be more economical than opting for tour packages. For the best prices on train tickets between Oslo and Bergen, book around three months in advance. In winter, keep in mind that daylight hours are limited to about six or seven hours a day.

Norway Travel Cost

Accommodation Costs

Accommodation in Norway varies widely depending on your budget and preferences. Budget travelers can find dormitory beds in hostels ranging from 250-400 NOK per night. Mid-range hotels typically cost 1,200-2,000 NOK per night for a double room, while luxury hotels can go up to 4,000 NOK or more per night. Alternative options like Airbnb or cabin rentals in the countryside start at around 800 NOK per night. Campsites are available for 200-400 NOK per night if you're traveling during warmer months.

Food and Dining Costs

Dining out in Norway is expensive due to high labor costs. A meal at a budget restaurant costs 150-250 NOK, while mid-range establishments charge 300-600 NOK for a three-course meal. Fast food options like burgers or pizza cost 100-200 NOK. For grocery shopping, expect to spend 500-800 NOK per week if you're cooking your meals. Local supermarkets like Rema 1000, Kiwi, and Coop have competitive prices. Alcohol is costly, with beer at bars averaging 90-120 NOK and a bottle of wine in restaurants costing 500 NOK or more.

Transportation Costs

Norway's transportation system is efficient but pricey. A single bus, tram, or metro ticket in cities like Oslo costs 38-42 NOK, with day passes ranging from 120-150 NOK. Taxis start at 100-120 NOK with an additional 15-20 NOK per kilometer. Train travel between cities, such as Oslo to Bergen, costs 500-1,000 NOK depending on the class and booking time. Domestic flights are frequent, averaging 800-1,500 NOK one-way. Renting a car costs 800-1,500 NOK per day, excluding fuel, which is approximately 25 NOK per liter.

Activity Costs

Popular attractions such as museums and galleries charge 100-250 NOK for entry. Guided tours, like fjord cruises, range from 600-1,200 NOK per person. Outdoor activities such as skiing cost 500-800 NOK for a day pass, with equipment rentals adding another 400-600 NOK. Hiking and exploring national parks are free but may require transportation costs to reach trailheads. Whale-watching tours cost 1,000-1,500 NOK, while Northern Lights excursions are priced at 1,000-2,500 NOK.

Miscellaneous Costs

Travel insurance is crucial and typically costs 50-100 NOK per day. SIM cards for local mobile data cost around 200-300 NOK, with data packages starting at 100 NOK. Souvenirs such as sweaters, trolls, or handmade crafts range from 200-1,000 NOK. Public restrooms usually charge 10-20 NOK, so carry some coins.

Daily Budget Estimates

- Budget Travelers: 800-1,200 NOK per day, covering hostels, public transportation, groceries, and free activities.
- Mid-Range Travelers: 2,000-3,500 NOK per day, including mid-range hotels, dining out, guided tours, and intercity transport.
- Luxury Travelers: 5,000 NOK or more per day for high-end accommodation, fine dining, private tours, and car rentals.

Tips for Saving Costs

- Use the Norwegian Public Transport App for discounts on public transportation.

- Travel off-peak (September–November or April–May) for reduced accommodation and activity costs.
- Cook your meals using local supermarket ingredients.
- Opt for budget airlines like Norwegian Air for domestic and international flights.
- Consider purchasing a Norway in a Nutshell package for bundled transportation and fjord tours.

Planning your budget thoughtfully ensures an unforgettable experience in Norway without overspending.

Tips for Travelers

Currency and Payment in Norway
Norway maintains its own currency, the Norwegian krone (NKr), even though neighboring countries have adopted the euro. When shopping, you'll typically see prices written as "Kr" followed by the amount, such as Kr 10, rather than the official NKr symbol.

Passport Requirements for U.S. Citizens
U.S. citizens, including infants, must have a valid passport to enter Norway for stays of up to three months. The passport should be valid for at least three months beyond your planned departure to avoid denial of entry.

Telephone and Communication Information
Norway's country code is 47, and all phone numbers consist of eight digits. There are no area codes. Numbers starting with 9 or 4 are mobile numbers, which tend to be more expensive to call. Numbers beginning with 82 cost extra, while toll-free numbers start with 800 or 810. Calls to numbers starting with 815 are charged NKr 1 per call.

Tipping Etiquette in Norway
Tipping is not as common in Norway due to higher wages compared to other countries. However, a 10% tip is customary at nicer restaurants. Taxi drivers generally don't expect tips, though rounding up the fare by NKr 10 is appreciated.

Oslo

Oslo is a blend of modern architecture and traditional charm. Although the city is known for its skyscrapers and international atmosphere, you can still find some of the quintessential Norwegian architecture in the city. The area around Damstredet and Telthusbakken features colorful, wooden houses from the 18th and 19th centuries. Additionally, Bygdøy's Norsk Folkemuseum offers a glimpse of Norway's past, complete with a traditional stave church.

Prepare for Unpredictable Weather

Norwegian weather can be highly unpredictable, especially in the mountains. Be prepared for sudden rain or cold, no matter the season. It's advisable to layer your clothing, starting with moisture-wicking fabrics, followed by a woolen layer for warmth, and finishing with a wind- and water-resistant jacket. In the mountains, sturdy hiking boots with a good grip are essential for navigating rocky trails.

Winter in Norway

The western coastal areas of Norway, like Stavanger, don't experience heavy snowfall due to the Gulf Stream, which keeps temperatures milder. While you may not see a winter wonderland, the fjords remain unfrozen, and you might spot snowcapped peaks in the distance. Fjord cruises are available year-round, offering a chance to witness Norway's winter landscapes.

Dining in Norway

Dining out in Norway can be expensive, so consider booking accommodations with kitchen access if you're on a budget. Dinner in restaurants typically costs between NKr 150 and NKr 400. Lunch is generally the least expensive meal, with costs ranging from NKr 30 to NKr 100 at kiosks and cafes. At sit-down restaurants, lunch can range from NKr 80 to NKr 180, depending on the dish and drinks. Look for specials, such as soup or salad with bread, which are often cheaper options. You can also save money by eating at less touristy establishments rather than those near major attractions.

The Northern Lights

The aurora borealis, a natural light display caused by solar particles colliding with Earth's atmosphere, is most visible during periods of high solar activity, which typically occur from autumn through early spring. While these stunning green (and sometimes purple) lights are a rare sight in the southern regions, they're a regular occurrence above the Arctic Circle. Tromsø and Alta are popular northern lights viewing spots, offering plenty of tours. For an exceptional chance, head to Svalbard, situated at 78° north, where conditions for witnessing the phenomenon are at their peak—weather permitting, of course.

Appreciating Norwegian Brands

Norwegians take pride in their unique culture and heritage, and supporting local brands like Helly Hansen and Devold shows an understanding of their national pride. While local brands are respected, praising Swedish giants like IKEA might not garner the same enthusiasm, given the friendly rivalry between the two countries. Acknowledging these distinctions can help you connect more deeply with locals.

Planning Your Ideal Road Trip Across Norway

Norway, with its stunning 25,148 km (15,626 miles) coastline, offers an incredible but demanding experience for road travelers. From the majestic fjords of the west to the charming fishing villages of the south, and the rugged islands north of the Arctic Circle, there's much to explore. Not to mention the vibrant cities like Oslo and Bergen, each offering their own unique attractions. How can you experience all of this in one unforgettable journey?

Choosing Your Starting Point

When planning a road trip in Norway, it's best to focus on one or two regions to fully immerse yourself in the experience. While driving the entire country is possible, it would require multiple days just to cover the distance from south to north. Rental cars in Norway can be expensive, particularly if you're planning on returning them in a different location. It's smarter to start in a well-connected city and choose a region to explore in detail. From Bergen, the western fjords are within easy reach, while Oslo offers quick access to the southern coastline. For those aiming to head further north, Bodø is a great starting point for a trip to the Lofoten Islands.

How Much Time to Set Aside

Norway's scenic roads come with their own challenges. Speed limits are relatively low, capping at 80 kph (50 mph), and highways are few and far between. The country's winding mountain roads and fjord-edge routes mean you'll cover less ground than expected each day. Instead of focusing on speed, consider taking the most scenic route, such as one of Norway's National Tourist Routes. Allow extra time for unplanned photo stops along the way, and be prepared to take ferries, which can add 30 to 60 minutes to your trip.

The Best Time to Go

For the most reliable weather, visit Norway between June and August. This is when the roads are most traveled, so be sure to book accommodations early, especially near popular destinations. Spring is beautiful too, with limited snow at lower elevations and great skiing in the mountains. Fall offers fewer crowds but lacks the appeal of ski resorts, as most haven't opened yet, and summer attractions are closed. Winter, while stunning, brings short days and cold, dark conditions, making it the most challenging time for a road trip.

Important Considerations During Your Trip

Even with clear skies, road conditions in Norway can change quickly due to floods, avalanches, or icy weather. Be prepared for occasional road closures that might leave you stranded for hours. Wildlife, especially moose and reindeer, can unexpectedly appear on the roads, as well as sheep wandering in rural areas. Don't forget that ferry rides across fjords will add extra time to your itinerary. However, with careful planning and attention to weather conditions, a road trip through Norway will undoubtedly be an unforgettable adventure.

Essential Packing Tips for Your Norway Trip

Packing for a trip to Norway requires careful consideration due to the country's unpredictable weather. Layering is essential, regardless of the season. Whether you're skiing in Lillehammer during winter or driving along the coast near Kristiansand on a summer day, packing wisely is key.

Clothing Essentials

Norwegians embrace the philosophy that there's no bad weather—only inadequate clothing. Prepare for sudden weather changes, and focus on layering. Start with a moisture-wicking base layer in the summer or thermal undergarments in the winter. Wool is a top choice for insulation, so consider packing a wool sweater or fleece jacket that works year-round. Summer nights can be chilly, so don't underestimate the need for warmth. Your outer layer should be waterproof, windproof, and insulated, especially for northern or mountainous regions. A hat, scarf, and gloves are essential in fall, winter, or spring. In summer, a good rain jacket and hiking pants will be beneficial, particularly around Bergen and the western fjords where rainfall is frequent.

Norwegians typically dress casually, even in restaurants, so you won't need to pack formal attire. A sweater will often suffice, and accessorizing with a stylish scarf can elevate your outfit without the need for anything fancy.

Footwear Recommendations

Proper footwear is crucial, especially if you plan to hike. High-quality waterproof hiking boots with good traction are essential to navigate Norway's often slippery mountain trails. For city excursions, a versatile pair of waterproof hiking shoes will save room in your luggage and provide comfort on urban streets. Avoid packing heels, as cobblestone streets and rugged terrain are not heel-friendly.

Essential Equipment

A waterproof daypack is necessary for all seasons. In summer, bring insect repellent and sunscreen, as Norway's cool breezes can mask the strength of the sun. If you're prone to motion sickness, pack medication, especially if you're taking ferries or winding mountain routes. Lastly, a reusable water bottle is highly recommended. Not only is Norway's tap water safe and free, but it's also delicious, making it a great resource for staying hydrated on your travels.

Unique Souvenirs from Norway

Convenient Tube Foods
Norwegians have perfected portable foods, especially in tube form, which are practical for outdoor adventures like hiking or skiing. Popular options include caviar, flavored cream cheese, and various condiments that can last up to two weeks without refrigeration, making them a convenient choice for active lifestyles.

Iconic Troll Figurines
Troll figures, sold in all shapes and sizes, are deeply rooted in Norwegian folklore. While modern souvenirs depict them humorously, traditional tales portray trolls as menacing and unattractive. These mythical beings gained fame through 19th-century collections by Asbjørnsen and Moe, Norway's equivalent of the Brothers Grimm.

Classic Cheese Slicer
Invented by Thor Bjørklund in the 1920s, the cheese slicer is a practical Norwegian creation inspired by woodworking tools. Despite resistance from cheese makers fearing reduced consumption, it became a household staple and a memorable gift for visitors.

Handcrafted Wooden Cups
Wooden coffee mugs, often crafted from birch or reindeer horn, are a testament to Scandinavian craftsmanship. These traditional cups, commonly used by hikers in Norway, are both practical and a charming keepsake.

Selbu Mittens
Renowned for their intricate black-and-white patterns, Selbu mittens have been a Norwegian knitting tradition for over 150 years. Originating from Selbu near Trondheim, they feature a distinctive eight-point star design and are widely available in souvenir shops.

Marius Sweaters
Introduced in the 1950s, Marius sweaters are Norway's most famous knitwear. Made of durable wool, these thick, hand-knit garments are not only stylish but practical, often replacing jackets in cold weather.

Akevitt
This traditional Norwegian spirit, made from potatoes and infused with herbs like dill and cardamom, is a staple for celebrations. Aged versions offer distinct flavors, and akevitt pairs well with authentic Norwegian dishes, making it a must-try for visitors.

Kvikk Lunsj Bars
Norway's take on the KitKat, Kvikk Lunsj is a beloved milk chocolate snack by Freia. Found in every supermarket, it's a popular treat for locals and visitors alike.

Mackerel in Tomato Sauce
Once central to Stavanger's fish-canning industry, canned mackerel in tomato sauce remains a lunchtime favorite in Norway. Though sardines were historically dominant, mackerel has become a modern staple.

Rosemaling Artwork
Rosemaling, a revived 19th-century folk art, features vibrant, decorative designs on wooden items like bowls and plates. These handcrafted pieces reflect Norway's artistic heritage and are perfect for bringing home a touch of tradition.

Delicacies to Try in Norway

Skoleboller Pastries
Known as "school buns," these custard-filled pastries topped with grated coconut are a sweet treat you can find in almost any café, making them a favorite for those with a sweet tooth.

Reindeer Dishes
A staple of Sámi culture, reindeer meat is served in northern Norway with mashed potatoes and lingonberry sauce. It's also enjoyed dried or as kebabs during festivals like Tromsø's SMAK in September.

Brown Cheese
Brunost, a caramelized goat cheese created in the 19th century, is a Norwegian favorite for sandwiches and waffles. Regional variations abound, and locals often recommend trying cheese from nearby farms.
Norwegian Culinary Specialties

King Crab Delicacies
Introduced to the Barents Sea in the 1960s by Soviet scientists, king crabs have become a Norwegian dining favorite. These sizable crustaceans are often served in soups or simply accompanied by bread and mayonnaise, showcasing their rich flavor.

Creamy Fish Soup
This hearty soup, featuring cod chunks and vegetables, is a national staple. Bergen offers a unique twist with salmon, halibut, or shrimp, making it a comforting winter dish perfect for warming up after braving the cold.

Norwegian Fish Cakes
Thinner and smaller than other versions, Norwegian fish cakes are a common roadside diner treat. Typically served with potatoes or in a bun, they are a quick, satisfying meal.

Fårikål Stew
As Norway's unofficial national dish, fårikål combines mutton and cabbage in a flavorful stew often enjoyed with bread and potatoes. It's particularly popular in autumn and pairs wonderfully with beer.

Lapskaus Stew
Adopted from northern Germany, lapskaus is a hearty stew with beef or pork, vegetables, and potatoes. This classic home-cooked dish complements local beers, offering a true taste of Norway.

Lefse Flatbread
Lefse, a thin potato flatbread, is commonly rolled with butter, sugar, and cinnamon for a sweet treat. Northern regions like Nordland feature a thicker variation, møsbrømlefse, made with brown cheese.

Norwegian Meatballs
Thicker and less round than Swedish meatballs, these are a staple of Norwegian cuisine. Served with mashed potatoes and brown gravy, they embody comfort food at its finest.

Traditional Stockfish
Stockfish, air-dried cod from northern Norway's Lofoten Islands, is a culinary tradition. Paired with vegetables and potatoes, this dish highlights Norway's fishing heritage.

Lutefisk Tradition
A Christmastime favorite, lutefisk is made from aged stockfish and lye, resulting in a gelatinous dish. While not for everyone, it remains a holiday staple often paired with white wine.

Ribbe for Christmas
Ribbe, roasted pork belly with a crispy crust, is a festive holiday dish. Served with potatoes, sour cabbage, and lingonberry sauce, it's a must-try for Christmas dinner.

Pinnekjøtt Feast
On Christmas Eve, many Norwegians enjoy pinnekjøtt, or "stick meat," consisting of lamb or mutton ribs. Traditionally served with potatoes, it's a beloved seasonal specialty.

> **Smalahove in Rural Norway**
> Smalahove, boiled sheep's head served with potatoes and mashed rutabaga, is a Christmas dish in rural western Norway. Though an acquired taste, it's steeped in cultural tradition.

Health and Emergency Contacts

Essential Norwegian Contact Information

Dialing Norway

To make international calls to Norway, use the country code +47 or 0047, followed by the recipient's number. Emergency services are accessible by dialing 110 for fire, 112 for police, 113 for ambulance, and 116117 for a doctor.

Air Travel

For air travel within and to Norway, Norwegian Airlines (phone: 21-49-00-15, website: norwegian.com), Scandinavian Airlines (phone: 21-89-64-00, website: flysas.com), and Widerøe (phone: 75-80-35-68, website: wideroe.no) are key carriers. Major airports include Bergen (phone: 67-03-15-55, website: airport-bergen.com), Kristiansand (phone: 67-03-03-30, website: avinor.no/en/airport/kristiansand-airport), Sandefjord (phone: 33-42-70-00, website: torp.no/en), Tromsø (phone: 67-03-46-00, website: avinor.no/en/airport/tromso-airport), and Trondheim (phone: 67-03-25-00, website: avinor.no/en/airport/trondheim-airport). For transfers, services like Flybussen (phone: 48-28-05-00, website: flybussen.no), Flytoget (phone: 23-15-90-00, website: flytoget.no/en), and Torp Express Buss (phone: 23-00-24-00, website: torp.no/en/transport/bus) are available.

Sea Travel

For travel by sea, contact Colorline (phone: 99-56-19-00, website: colorline.com/denmark-norway), DFDS Scandinavian Seaways (Oslo office: phone: 23-10-68-00, website: dfds.no), or Hurtigruten (phone: 810-30-000, website: hurtigruten.com).

Bus Services

Norwegian bus operators include Nettbuss (phone: 04-070-5070, website: nettbuss.no), Nor-Way Bussekspress (phone: 02-231-3150, website: nor-way.no), and Lavprisekspressen (phone: 06-798-0480, website:

lavprisekspressen.no).

Car Assistance

For car-related assistance, Falck Global Assistance is available at phone: 21-49-24-15 and website: falck.no.

Train Travel

Train travel is supported by Entur (phone: 06/127-9088, website: entur.org) and Interrail (phone: 880-0161-05, website: interrail.eu).

U.S. Embassy

The U.S. Embassy in Norway is located at Morgedalsvegen 36 (phone: 21-30-85-40, website: no.usembassy.gov). The Royal Norwegian Embassy in Washington, D.C., can be reached at 2720 34th Street NW (phone: 202-333-6000, website: norway.no/en/usa).

Visitor Information

Tourist assistance is available through Fjord Norway (Stavanger office: website: fjordnorway.com), Norway National Parks (website: nasjonalparkriket.no/en), and Visit Norway (website: visitnorway.com).

QUICK NOTE

"I hope this chapter proved informative. Your feedback on the book thus far is highly valued and will be used to enhance future editions. Please take a moment to share your thoughts by dropping a review on Amazon. Thank you, and enjoy the rest of the book."

CONCLUSION

Thank you for choosing this travel guide to Norway. Your decision to explore this extraordinary country reflects a spirit of adventure and a curiosity for the world's most awe-inspiring landscapes. I hope the information and insights in these pages have equipped you to make the most of your journey, from the majestic fjords and vibrant cities to the rich cultural traditions and outdoor wonders.

As you embark on your Norwegian adventure, may you find joy in every experience—whether it's a quiet moment under the Northern Lights, the thrill of hiking a breathtaking trail, or the simple pleasure of connecting with the warm and welcoming people of Norway.

Safe travels, and may Norway's magic leave an unforgettable imprint on your heart. Happy exploring!

SCAN THE QR CODE BELOW TO GET THE BONUS.

SCAN QR CODE

1. Open your phone's camera.
2. Aim at the QR code.
3. Wait for it to be recognized.
4. Tap if you need to scan.
5. Type 0$ under the (Name a fair-priced) search bar.
6. Click, I want this.

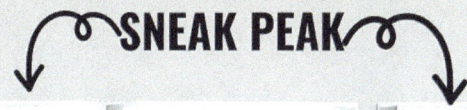

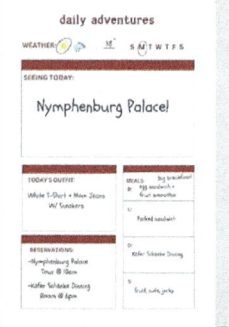

SNEAK PEAK

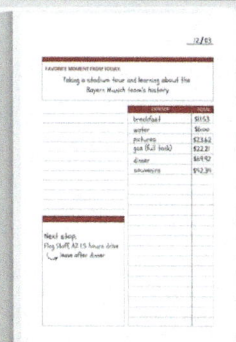

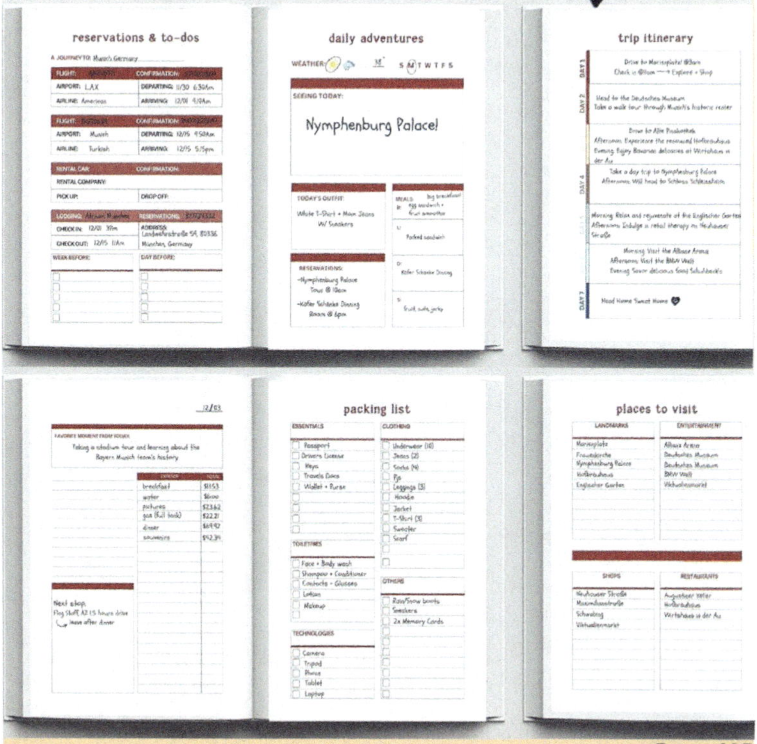

Page 195

Made in the USA
Las Vegas, NV
22 March 2025